LOVE, LOSS AND THE LIGHT WITHIN

Prajwal Ghogare

ISBN
Paperback: 979-8-89744-958-3
Hardcase: 979-8-89906-830-0

Chhatrapati Shivaji Maharaj's
vision, leadership, and sacrifice will
continue to inspire generations. This
writing is humbly offered at his feet.
Jai Bhavani*, **Jai Shivaji!***

Before You Begin

Writing this book has been a journey, one that has taken me over two years. There were times when I wrote with passion, and there were times when I left it unfinished, lost in the chaos of life. But then, one incident changed everything. It became the turning point that pushed me to finally complete what I had started. It's funny how life gives us unexpected reasons to finish what we once left behind, and for me, this book was one of those things.

As human beings, we all experience similar emotions, even if our stories are different. We love deeply, we expect things from others, we break when things don't go as we hoped, and in the end, we all want to be happy. This book is built on these fourimportant aspects of lifelove, expectations, heartbreak, and happiness. Love is beautiful, but what is love, really? Expectations are natural, but what should we expect, and from whom? Heartbreak is painful, but how do we heal? And most importantly, happiness is it something we find, or something we create? These are the questions I have explored in these pages, not through theories, but through emotions, experiences, and reflections on life itself.

This book will help you understand the true meaning of love and how to love in a way that brings joy rather than pain. It will guide you on managing expectations, teaching you what to expect, from whom, and how to handle disappointments.

It will show you how to heal from heartbreak, to let go of the past, and to move forward with strength. And most importantly, it will help you explore happiness which is most important aspect in life.

Before you begin, there's something important I want to share is that one of the biggest lessons I have learned is that not everyone deserves our love. We often give so much of ourselves to people who don't value it, who take us for granted, and who fail to understand the depth of our emotions. Love is precious, and it should be given to those who truly deserve it. We hold on, hoping they will change, believing that if we love them enough, they will finally understand. But in reality we lose ourselves in the process of making someone else feel whole. Love is one of the most precious gifts we have to offer, and it should be given to those who value, respect, and nurture it. It should be shared with those who see our worth, who reciprocate our efforts, and who make us feel cherished rather than questioning our place in their lives. Love wisely and recognize who truly deserves a place in our hearts.

See lifeis not always fair. It will test you, challenge you, and at times, break you. There will be moments when you will feel the urge to give up on kindness, to let go of your morals, and to become the person the world has been unkind to. But even in those moments, remember your choices define you. No matter how cruel world is to you, choose to be good. There were many times when I had every reason to become a villain, to let my pain turn into anger, but I chose to be a hero. And if there's one thing I hope this book reminds you of, it's that no matter what life throws at you, you always have the power to choose who you become.

Lastly this book is a reflection of emotions that we all go through at some point in life. I hope that as you read, you find pieces of yourself in these pages. These pages hold feelings, lessons, and realizations that many of us have lived through but often struggle to put into words. I hope you see your own emotions, your own experiences, and your own journey reflected here. And more than anything, I hope that by the time you reach the last page, you feel a little lighter, a little wiser, and a little more at peace with yourself.

Thank you for being a part of this journey.

Happy reading!

–Prajwal

*We love. We expect. We break. We heal.
And somewhere between these
moments, we find ourselves.*

Table of Contents

1) Love

I) Defining Love

(*Love is simply LOVE*)

Nobody has ever fully understood love, may be because it's different for everyone. Some say it brings happiness, peace, and stability into their lives, while others describe it as the most hurtful and complex emotion that they have ever experienced. Love, when found in its true form, can feel like a victory, but when it goes wrong, it can seem like a failure of a lifetime. Love can be a source of immense joy or deep sorrow, an inspiration or a challenge, a binding force or a liberating experience. Love can be anything, and that's why no one truly understands it. It has power to make us feel joy, pain, to bring us together or to tear us apart. Love is powerful and mysterious, and very hard to define.

Love is feeling, an emotion it cannot be seen or even touched, it can only be felt with the heart. Without love, our lives would have no meaning; we would be like robots, going through the motions without any feeling. Our ability to love is what sets us apart from other animals. Love doesn't cost anything, but it can give us everything. You can't measure love with your eyes or hands, but you can always feel its warmth and comfort deep inside. Being always there for someone is what love is all about. It means putting in the effort, going the extra mile for someone, and caring deeply for them. Love is feeling presence of someone even when they are not physically present. When you love someone, you show them through your actions. Love about supporting them when they need it, offering a shoulder to cry on, and celebrating their successes like our own. Love can be as simple as staying up late to talk to them when they've had a bad day. It's also about understanding when they're feeling down, and doing something special just to make them smile. Love is about the comfort of knowing that someone is always there for you. Love is the small acts of kindness that someone does for you or you do it for someone every day to show how much you care.

Now let's dive more deep into love. There are endless ways how everyone sees love; let's discover and try to understand them together, one form of love with paragraph at a time, because love is about doing things together.

We live in a generation where love feels very different from what it used to be. Love today is a very different entity compared to what we've read in ancient tales, heard in timeless legends, or seen in classic movies. Today, while love still holds a powerful place in our lives, its meaning has evolved, reflecting the world we live in. So if I were to explain love in today's generation, then love is like the feeling of high you get from drugs or alcohol. It's that rush of euphoria when you're with that special one, a mix feeling of happiness and excitement that feels like adrenaline pumping through your veins. Love makes your heart race, and every moment that you spent together feels like a thrilling adventure. If you give your attention, then you will understand that initially love feels like a rush, and being with the person you love makes your heart beat faster than normal, your body also feels a bit unusual. You feel butterflies in your stomach and time slows down when you're together, and the world seems a brighter place, so *love is rush.*

We often hear or are told that love is a process of give and take. But one thing that's also true is that there is no love without sacrifice. True love goes beyond just giving and receiving; it involves sacrifice. When you truly love someone, you are willing to give up something important for their happiness. Sacrificing for someone you love is one of the most beautiful parts of love. It isn't something you plan or think about; it happens naturally, like a river flowing towards the ocean. The person who sacrifices doesn't even realize they are giving up something, because their heart is so full of love. We live in a world where many people just care about themselves and nothing else. And in such a selfish world, if someone puts you before themselves, it means they love you more than anyone else. This kind of love is special and rare. It shows that the person truly values you and your happiness. Sacrifice in love can be anything like investing time, efforts, and putting your partner's needs and well-being ahead of your own and making compromises for the sake of the relationship. Sacrifice develops trust, intimacy, and respect in relationship. When you sacrifices for your partner it strengthens the trust between you and your partner and also the sense of security. But for a healthy relationship it's important to maintain balance of give and take. When I say you have to maintain balance of give and take, what I am trying to say is that sacrifice should not be one-sided or it will lead to the feelings of resentment. Both partners should be willing to make sacrifices for each other not just the one. This mutual effort shows that both people value and care for one another equally. If only one person is always making sacrifices, it can create an imbalance in relationship. Always remember, when you're in a committed relationship, you have to make sacrifices for the person you love because you're a team now. Being in a relationship means making decisions together and recognizing that neither person is bigger or more important than the other. You both are equal. Love is always greater than the peoples in it, even bible says that sacrifice as the greatest display of love for others. At last love is not just about what you receive, but also about what you are willing to give up for the one you love. *Love is sacrifice.*

When we talk about love we mostly focus on romantic relationships only. However that's not the only kind of love, one integral kind of love that we have in life is called friendship. Very few people are lucky enough to find both romantic love and friendship in one person, creating a strong bond that can last a lifetime, because love is a friendship and in most of the cases love starts with a friendship. A friend is someone you can trust and rely on in good and bad times. You share laughter, secrets, and support you when you need it most. A true friend listens without judging, and stands by your side through life's ups and downs. And we search these qualities in that special person too, so it's fair to say that love is built on a strong foundation of friendship. Because when two people share common interests, trust, and support for each other, they create a deep connection. This closeness can naturally grow into love, as they realize they not only enjoy being together but also care deeply for one another. Your partner should be your best friend, someone you can trust and share everything with. But also it's important that even with a strong friendship, the love between you should always be there and remain special. I feel love is more special when it starts with friendship because friendship brings trust and understanding. When you start as friends, you learn about each other's hopes, dreams, insecurities which will help your relationship to be peaceful and more beautiful. Remember Love is not just about romance; it's about being each other's best friend. So *love is a friendship.*

In love, I feel loyalty is everything. Loyalty isn't something you simply display; it's in love itself, by saying this what I am trying to say is that if you love someone then you must be loyal to that person even without that person asking for it. Loyalty is responsibility. Relationship will not survive if there is no loyalty in it. Relationships and loyalty go hand in hand. It may have become the most ignored notion today, but loyalty is all that binds you together no matter which era we are living in. Loyalty is the glue that holds the relationship tighter. It means being truthful and transparent with your partner about your feelings, intentions, and actions. Loyalty means knowing the boundaries you can never cross, staying within limits and honouring the trust others have placed in you, even when it's difficult. If you give your firm loyalty to the person you love, then you have given that person everything. Be someone whom people can trust, because people fade, looks fade but loyalty stays forever. *Love is loyalty.*

When you love someone then you open your heart and you let that person to see the real you. When you love someone, you share your deepest feelings, fears, secrets, insecurities and dreams. This means you show the person you love your true self, even if it feels a bit scary. This means we are vulnerable in love, being vulnerable in love means you're willing to take risks, it means you are willing to get hurt or rejected but you still choose to be honest and open to that person. Vulnerability not just keeps us honest with our partner but also with ourselves, it breaks down walls and most certainly avoids miscommunication and misunderstandings, and allows us to be wholly ourselves. If you don't allow yourself to be vulnerable, then you can't expect your partner to understand what you need and want from them. Love finds its true strength in vulnerability. *Love is being vulnerable.*

Today we live in a very selfish and self-centred world where many people are only driven by the personal gain. I mean we do have some special people around us whom we love, take care of but we hardly ignore our own needs and desires in the process. This raises the question, does unconditional love really exist? Or should it exist? In an ideal world, it should.

Where we love others fully without any conditions or expectations. But we don't live in an ideal world. No matter how beautiful unconditional love sounds but I feel there should not be an unconditional love it will only make things poor for your relationship. A relationship involves two people who are equally important to its success. When one person loves unconditionally, it leads to an imbalance where only one person feels happy or fulfilled. Love is not just about making one person happy, both people are important, and everyone deserves to be happy. Love is collective responsibility of both the individuals to work together to bring happiness in each other's lives. If only one person is making all the efforts in a relationship, it will eventually fail. A healthy relationship needs both people to contribute equally. I feel love should always be conditional, it may sound surprising but its healthy approach to relationships. Conditional love doesn't mean that you love someone less; it only means that you love yourself and the other person too. When I say love should have conditions I am not talking about the materialistic conditions, the certain conditions I am talking about are mutual respect, honesty, and kindness. Because these conditions will helps to ensure that both people in the relationship are treated well and that their needs are met. Setting boundaries and conditions will only make your relationship better. Remember love is a partnership where both people are important. *Love is conditional.*

The first thing I said about love is that love is simple. However, after so many definitions, love can seem quite complicated.

Love is fundamentally about perspective; everyone experiences and feels love in their own unique way. As I mentioned earlier, love varies for different people and can mean different things to different individuals.

Yes, love has many forms, experiences and expressions there isn't just one unique definition for it. Despite exploring many different forms and interpretations of love, I will conclude this section as love being simple. Yes, love can be as simple as calling someone your brother or sister, even if they are not your real siblings. Love goes beyond the traditions and definitions. Love is about the emotional ties and support you give to others, making every moment together feel like you're among loved ones. Love is simple. It's not about grand gestures or complicated expressions; it's about the small, everyday moments that build a connection. Love is something where actions speak louder than any elaborated plans or gifts. At its core, love is about being present, being kind to that person, when we focus on these straight forward things, then love becomes clear and effortless, a gentle reminder that the best relationships are built on simple, honest moments of togetherness. And Love doesn't need anything extra to be love.

Love doesn't need friendship to be love.

Love doesn't need sacrifices to be love.

Love doesn't need validation to be love.

Love doesn't need promises to be love.

Love doesn't need conditions to be love.

Love doesn't need perfection to be love.

Love doesn't need physical attraction to be love.

Love is simply love.

II) Keeping The Flame Alive

(Real love shines through in your commitment to stay the same for each other, no matter what changes come your way.)

In relationships, love is like a bright thread that ties together happy and caring moments. But just like anything valuable, love also needs attention and effort to stay strong and lasting. Without attention the love will eventually fail. It's easy to fall in love or to get in a relationship but keeping that love strong and fresh over time is much more challenging. It requires effort and commitment to sustain the connection and to keep the flame of your relationship alive.

Love, in its early stages, often feels easy and exciting. But as time goes on, keeping the spark alive can be harder with everyday routines and pressures. Love is not just a feeling it's something that needs constant efforts and growth from both partners. Love is like a flame but it doesn't stay bright on its own. Just like any flame, it needs regular care and attention to stay alive and glowing. Love is not about how many days, months, or years you have been together. Love is about how much you love each other every single day.

As I mentioned earlier that love, in its purest form, is one of the most beautiful experiences life has to offer. Love is beautiful because it is ever-evolving, ever-growing. It is a journey that demands commitment, understanding, and a willingness to keep the flame alive, even when the path is challenging. But keeping the flame alive in love requires conscious effort and understanding. Understanding plays huge role in relationship to succeed. Understanding is the silent force that keeps the relationship going. When you truly understand your partner, you see beyond words and actions; we grasp the emotions, fears, and dreams that drive them. I feel more than anything understanding is a choice you have to make every day to see and appreciate our partner for who they truly are. We humans often see the world only from our own perspective. We believe that our thoughts, opinions, and decisions are always right. We live based on our assumptions rather than facing reality, we are convinced that our perspective is the only correct one. But let's be honest with ourselves, we must acknowledge that we cannot be always right. That's where understanding plays such a crucial role in our lives. It means stepping outside of our own mind set and putting ourselves in our partner's shoes, and to see the world from their perspective. When we see the world from our partner's perspective, we begin to understand the circumstances and motivations behind their actions. We realize that their actions may not always be about us, but could be because of their internal struggles, needs and the emotions that our partner carries. Life is a journey of constant change, and with it, people in a relationship also grow and evolve. So you have to be understanding and you must keep patience to accept and adapt to these changes both in ourselves and our partner. It means giving each other the space to grow, make mistakes, and learn without fear of judgment or rejection. It is in this shared understanding that love finds its strength, beauty, and longevity. To love and to make your love work you must be an understanding human. The world becomes more beautiful when we see it through our partner's eyes, not just our own.

Love is all about the small things that we remember and are willing to do for the person we love, because relationship isn't always about grand gestures, sometimes it's the simple, sincere acts of kindness like remembering a special detail or offering a helping hand that truly convey our love. These Small gestures, like making your partner's favourite coffee, leaving a sweet note might seem minor, but they carry immense meaning. Love is best expressed through actions rather than words. At the beginning of a relationship, it's common to spend a lot of time together and enjoying each other's company. However, as time goes on, it's easy to fall into the trap of taking the other person for granted, and the frequency of shared time may also decrease. It's crucial to remember that spending quality time together remains essential to maintaining a strong, healthy relationship. Spending quality time together, even small, can have a big impact. Whether it's sharing a meal, taking a walk, or simply sitting together, these moments of connection create memories. No matter how busy you are or how challenging it may be to find time, it's essential to make an effort for the person you love. Your partner deserves and has a rightful claim on your time, as you have chosen to spend your life together. By making time and doing small things for your partner, for your relationship you show how much your relationship matters and how committed you are to it.

See love is more than just a feeling; it's a responsibility. Just like brushing your teeth, you have to take care of your relationship regularly. When you love someone, you are not only sharing happiness but also taking care of their emotions, their trust, and their well-being. Being responsible in love means making an effort every day. This includes doing small, caring things and being there for each other. As is said small things make big difference in relationships so take time to express your love and appreciation every day. Remember, love needs consistent attention. Just as you make time for daily routines like eating or exercising, make time for your partner as well. This daily commitment means you value and appreciate them. Make love a daily habit, nurture your relationship, build trust, and ensure that your partner feel appreciated and valued every day. This commitment and responsibility you take helps you to keep the flame of your love burning brightly and ensures a strong, lasting connection.

Love isn't one-size-fits-all. The most important thing in a relationship is to understand each other's love language because everyone expresses and receives love in different ways and it may not always match how you express or expect love. For some, love might be shown through words of affirmation, while others might feel most loved through acts of service, quality time, physical touch, or receiving gifts. If you don't take the time to learn how your partner feels and shows love, there can be misunderstandings and unmet needs, even when love is there. Every person has their own way of expressing love. Understanding how your partner shows love is important for maintaining a peaceful and happy relationship. If you don't recognize these signs of love from your partner, you might feel unappreciated or misunderstood, even though they are showing love in their own way. By learning how your partner expresses their feelings, you can avoid unnecessary misunderstandings and create a deeper bond. You must understand that everyone brings different things to a relationship, and it's important to recognize and be grateful for those unique qualities. Each person has their own strengths, experiences, and ways of contributing to the relationship. One person might bring kindness and emotional support, while the other may offer stability or practical help. These differences are what make a relationship balanced and strong. So take time to appreciate what your partner brings, instead of focusing on what might be missing, because there will always be a missing pieces. Remember In the end, love is not about perfection, but about appreciating the beauty in each other's unique qualities. True love is when we are thankful for the little things & everything that the other person has to offer.

Another myth that we have heard about love is that love is about finding the right person or there is right person for everyone in the world. But in reality love isn't just about finding the perfect or right person; it's about becoming a better person yourself. In a relationship, it's important to grow and improve, not just for your partner, but for yourself as well. To keep the flame alive in love means we have to constantly work on ourselves, it's about being aware of our flaws, accepting them, and striving to improve, so we can contribute to a healthy, lasting partnership. No one is perfect in the world, so you may never find the perfect partner and expecting someone to be flawless or perfect always leads to disappointment as no one is perfect. Instead of searching perfection in your partner focus on becoming the best that partner you can be. When you work on yourself, you bring positive energy to the relationship, making it stronger and more fulfilling. One should never focus on what the other person lacks, instead focus on what you can give to that person and when both people show this kind of attitude in a relationship and focus on growing and becoming better, love lasts longer and becomes deeper. Love is about two imperfect people growing together, supporting each other through life's ups and downs. Being the perfect partner isn't about never making mistakes, but about being willing to grow, learn, and improve for the sake of the relationship. In the end, love isn't about finding perfection, rather it's about focusing on growth and giving your best to the relationship.

Be the giving partner in relationship without always expecting something in return. *Love grows through efforts, not through perfection.*

In an ideal relationship, one of the most important things you can do is honour the person you love. Because love is about respect, appreciation, and treating your partner with kindness. When you truly love someone, you don't take them for granted. You value their presence, their feelings, and their efforts. Honouring someone means showing them deep respect and valuing their worth. Honouring your partner is one of the most essential things to do in relationship. When both partners show respect and appreciation for one another, it builds a strong sense of trust. In relationship you have to respect each other's feelings, opinions, and needs this will help to prevent misunderstandings. When you honour each other, you strengthen your emotional connection and makes both partners feel valued and loved. Your acts may seem small but it can have big impact on your partner. Always show kindness, consideration to your partner to make them feel important because that person deserves all your heart. In conclusion, honouring each other is essential for a lasting and happy relationship. It means truly valuing and respecting one another through kind actions and words. Honouring each other creates a supportive environment where both people can grow and be happy together, helping the relationship last for a lifetime.

As I mentioned earlier, true love doesn't depend on who the person is or what they can give you. It means loving someone deeply without expecting anything in return. Love is about loving them for who they are. Love is a strong and lasting bond that doesn't change with circumstances or demands. As I conclude this section, it's important to acknowledge that keeping the flame of love alive in today's world can be challenging. With busy lives, external pressures, and constant distractions, maintaining a strong relationship requires constant efforts and commitment. However, if you truly love your partner, keeping that love alive becomes much easier. The key is having the willpower and determination to nurture your relationship and make it last.

Love is not something that changes with circumstances, nor does it fade when challenges arise. When you truly love someone then you must stay committed through every season of life. Love means standing by each other, through the joys and the struggles, the moments of happiness and the challenges that life brings. It's about choosing your partner every day. Remember true love lasts for lifetime, love should not look for better, for richer, if you truly love you have to hold, not to give up till death does its part. If you are with the right person, someone who gives their heart, their time, and their effort to make the relationship stronger you owe them the same dedication in return. But to love last for lifetime you have to be committed to yourself more than your partner. You must commit to never letting go of the person you love, to always be there when they need you, and to stay loyal no matter what. It's a promise to stand by their side, to remain faithful, and to make sure they feel valued and loved. Love isn't always easy, but if you're committed to never giving up, then love does lasts forever. Love thrives when both people make the relationship a priority, nurture it with kindness, and remain dedicated even through the tough times.

Remember: *Love isn't just about finding someone you can live with; it's about finding someone you can't imagine living without. Keep the flame alive by always choosing love.*

III) Overcoming Obstacles

(Love is not about being perfect, but about being present every time)

Life is full of challenges, and obstacles are a part of every journey, whether personal or professional. But success in anything is not about avoiding difficulties; it's about refusing to give up, no matter how hard things get. Love, while it's beautiful and fulfilling, often faces challenges that test its strength. Obstacles in love are a natural part of any relationship, but they don't have to be barriers to your happiness. These obstacles can come in many forms like misunderstandings, differences in values, or the demands of daily life. However, it is how we handle these challenges that truly defines the depth of our love. Overcoming obstacles in love requires patience, communication, and a shared commitment to growing together. By facing difficulties together, communicating openly, and supporting each other through tough times, we not only overcome obstacles but also strengthen our bond. Love grows when both partners are willing to sail through these challenges and obstacles with patience, understanding, and resilience.

See things are never the same; they often get tough, and when things do get tough then it is a natural human tendency to walk away when faced with challenges. Because it feels like an escape from the pain, stress, and uncertainty. But leaving can never solve the problem it just delays it. No matter whatever you are going through leaving can never be an option because it takes the opportunity to grow and learn from our struggles. One of the biggest truths about love is that it will always go through hard times. And when things do get tough, don't walk away, because real love isn't about leaving when challenges arise. True love is about staying, facing the difficulties together, and working through the struggles. It's about finding ways to grow stronger as a couple. Obstacles are inevitable in any relationship. They can come in the form of misunderstandings, differences in opinions, or life circumstances that challenge your connection. However, love is not defined by the absence of problems but by the willingness to overcome them. In moments of conflict or hardship, it's easy to feel like giving up is the only way out. But ideal relationship is where both partners are committed to the relationship, where they will always choose to face challenges side by side, rather than running in opposite directions. Leaving may seem like a quick solution, but it only leads to regret. Staying through tough times shows the depth of your commitment. It's easy to love someone when everything is going well, but true love shines brightest in difficult times. When you stay and work through issues, you not only grow as a couple but also as individuals.

Love is built on trust and understanding. Every time you face an obstacle and come out stronger, you build more trust in each other. The foundation of overcoming any obstacle is open and honest communication. Sometimes, the issue may just be a misunderstanding that can be resolved with a simple conversation. We live in a fast-paced generation where we expect everything to happen in the blink of an eye. But love doesn't work that way it requires time and patience. You must understand that not every problem will be solved overnight. It takes time to heal, to understand, and to change. Be patient with your partner and with yourself. Growth is a process, and the results are worth waiting for.

In love, leaving should never be the first option. Challenges are not reasons to give up, but opportunities to strengthen the bond between you and your partner. When both people are committed to making it work, even the toughest obstacles can be overcome. Remember once you find true love and right person by your side then giving up is no longer an option.

Who doesn't make mistakes? Everyone does, right? It's part of being human. We're not perfect, and we never will be. Mistakes are simply part of the journey. They happen when we're learning, growing, or even when we're just trying to do our best. In relationships, this is especially true. No matter how much we love someone, there will be times when we hurt them, disappoint them, or let them down. And they'll do the same to us. But what's important to remember is that mistakes don't define us. What truly matters is how we respond to them. In love and relationships, its important to understand that mistakes are part of the process and they will only help us become more patient and forgiving. As mistakes are a natural part of being human, it makes forgiveness essential in any relationship. Forgiveness in love is not just about saying "I forgive you" or letting go of hurt. It has much more deeper meaning than that. Forgiveness means understanding. It's about seeing the other person's flaws, mistakes and choosing to respond with empathy instead of fighting with them. In any relationship, whether it's with a partner, a family member, or a close friend, misunderstandings and making mistakes are inevitable. We are all imperfect. We must understand that everyone is human, and we all have our own struggles and perspective. When we understand the struggles of our partner and why they acted the way they did, then it becomes easier to forgive them. It's important to forgive but that doesn't mean justifying hurtful behaviour, it only means looking beyond the immediate pain. Forgiveness is also an act of self-love because holding onto anger only deepens our wound. It keeps us stuck in the past. But when we forgive, we release that weight and free ourselves to heal and move forward.

While forgiving is important and act of kindness, it's also essential to understand that not every mistake is forgivable. Forgiveness does not mean allowing someone to continually hurt or disrespect you. There are certain actions that can break the trust in a relationship to a point where forgiveness does not make any sense. In my opinion, acts of betrayal, dishonesty, and intentional lying do not deserve forgiveness, because trust is the foundation of any relationship, and once it's broken, it's incredibly difficult to rebuild. Some people believe in giving second chances, but when it comes to lying or betrayal, I believe it's different. Once someone has proven that they're willing to deceive you, it's hard to trust that they won't do it again. As the saying goes, Fool me once, shame on you, fool me twice, shame on me. Trust is fragile. Once broken, it's hard to rebuild, and not everyone deserves that chance. A relationship without trust is like a house without a strong foundation it can't stand for long.

In the end, it's important to forgive people but it's equally important to be wise about who we choose to forgive. Forgiveness is a gift, and like any gift, we get to decide who receives it. Be kind, but be wise. Forgive people, but choose carefully when deciding who is worthy of rebuilding trust and continuing the relationship. Not everyone deserves a second chance, and it's perfectly okay to protect yourself from those who don't value your trust.

Life, as we know it, is never without challenges. We all had problems at different points in our journey, whether it's with our families, with our best friends, or even at work. Because relationships involve emotions, expectations, and misunderstandings. When two or more people come together, conflicts will always be there because we're all different and we all carry our own set of beliefs, habits, and past experiences.

Now, if you consider your own life. You've had disagreements with your family at some point, maybe a fallout with a best friend, or issues with colleagues. Because we all make mistakes, have bad days and no matter how perfect life is going we will still face problems at some point. Problems are simply part of being human. So why a romantic relationship should be any different? Why things should always have to be great or perfect in a romantic relationship? I feel that a relationship free from problems is an illusion. It can never exist. In my opinion there is no such a thing called perfect couple. I know we've all seen that in movies, read about it in books, or maybe even looked at other couples. But the truth is, no relationship is flawless. The only thing that is guaranteed in relationship is that there will always be problems. This isn't because of you and your partner are not trying hard enough or because you guys are not compatible, it's just because we are humans. And we carry our imperfections into the relationship. Life itself is unpredictable, and relationships are no different. You might try to do everything right and be the best version of yourself, but still you will still face disagreements, misunderstandings, and go through difficult times. It's just part of the journey. But here one thing that we must understand that having problems in a relationship is very normal thing it doesn't make your relationship any less valuable. In fact, how you deal with those problems does make a lot of difference. You should stop expecting everything to be smooth all the time. Instead, understand that every relationship has its ups and downs, and that's okay. A strong relationship is where you don't avoid problems but fight against them together side by side. Don't chase perfection in relationship, your goal should be understanding, building patience, and growth. We think that solving problems requires big actions or solutions, but often, the answer is much simpler, you just have to stop and listen. When listen to someone, you understand what they're feeling and experiencing. Because deep down, we all want to be understood.

So yes, no matter how much you try, and no matter how much your partner tries, there will always be problems. But problems don't define your relationship, how you overcome those does. Remember it's not about finding someone with whom you'll never have problems. It's about finding someone who's worth fighting through the problems.

Nowadays many relationships suffer not because of a lack of love, but because of insecurity. Insecurity creates doubt, fear, and unnecessary conflicts, making even the strongest bonds feel fragile. Your lover should not be insecure. Insecurity is not good in a relationship, that's what we've been told our whole lives. Insecurity is often seen as something negative or a sign of weakness in relationships. But in my opinion insecurity is not an obstacle in love actually it's a sign of deep love and care. When you love someone so much then the fear of losing that person will always be there, the more you love someone the more you will be insecure towards them. I feel that insecurity is the highest form of love because it shows vulnerability. A person who is insecure is willing to let down their guard and reveal the parts of themselves that most people usually keep hidden. By doing this, they take a risk, to face judgment or criticism, just for the sake of the relationship. Being insecure doesn't mean they are weak, it means they care so much about the relationship that they're willing to face uncomfortable feelings and be honest about them.

Yes, insecurity does come out of love. But like anything in life, too much of it can be harmful. So where do you draw the line? If someone has consistently shown you love, honesty, and loyalty, if they've never given you a reason to doubt them then there should be no space for insecurity. Trust is built over time, and once someone earns it, you shouldn't let unnecessary fears hamper your relationship. In only these cases, insecurity becomes toxic no matter how much you love your partner. On the other hand, if someone has broken your trust, if they've lied and betrayed you then that insecurity is harder to shake off because the trust that was once there has been damaged. Even if you choose to forgive them, the fear that they might hurt you again will always be there. Trust is the foundation of a strong relationship. It makes two people to feel safe and secure with each other. But once trust is shattered, it doesn't magically reappear overnight. It takes a lot of time and effort to rebuild it. That's why loyalty is one of the most valuable things you can offer in relationship. Be trustworthy. When you give your partner the gift of loyalty, you give them everything.

Remember it's going to be hard but be loyal no matter how hard it gets. It's the best thing you can give in any relationship. Where there is loyalty there is no space for toxic insecurity.

Change is also often seen as an obstacle in relationships. It's said that you should love someone just the way they are, without wanting them to change. While this sounds nice, the truth of life is everything changes. We grow and evolve, and so do our relationships. Think about who you were a year ago. You've changed in many ways. You've learned new things, faced challenges, or even discovered new passions. Growth and change is a natural part of being human. We're not meant to stay the same forever. In relationships, this evolution is important. As you change, so does your connection with your partner. Your viewpoints change, or you adapt to life's ups and downs. You and your partner have to adjust to each other's growth. You can't expect your partner to stay the same forever. People go through different experiences that shape who they are. Accept that change because its part of life, accepting it only strengthens your bond. Love is not just about accepting each other as you are today; it's also about being excited for who you will become tomorrow.

Another common obstacle in relationships is conflict. Sometimes, your partner may not be happy about certain habits or behaviours you have. You might think that your partner is being toxic or trying to control you. But it's important to look at the situation from a different angle. Love often means making adjustments for each other. This doesn't mean you have to change who you are completely, but being open to change. When your partner shares their feelings about something that bothers them, it's usually because they want relationship to be better. You have to let go of certain things about yourself for the sake of your partner and the relationship. Letting go can be tough. Because you are giving up certain habits, ways of thinking. This doesn't mean you're losing a part of yourself; it means you're showing love and respect for your partner. Relationship are mostly about compromise. Compromise means finding a middle ground where both people feel heard and respected. Give and take is what keeps the relationship healthy.

In the end love is not about avoiding obstacles but about learning from them. You may not find perfect solutions; but you will certainly find a way forward together. If both people are willing to put in the effort, any obstacle can be overcome.

Remember: *So fight for your love, if the person is worth fighting for.*

IV) Growing Together

(When two hearts grow together, no distance, no time, and no challenge can break them apart.)

As I said this earlier that love is not just about being with someone, nor just a feeling it's a continuous journey of growing together. In simple words when two hearts come together, they plant the seed of a relationship. But like any seed in garden, this seed of love also requires care, attention, and time to grow. Growing together simply means nurturing each other, learning from the ups and downs along the way. It's about becoming better individuals and a stronger couple by each passing day. Because love is commitment of being together and growing together.

The first and one of the most important factors in growing together as a couple is having effective communication with your partner. Communication is the foundation of any strong relationship. Without good communication, no relationship can survive for the longer period, without it misunderstandings can easily arise, and small issues turn can into bigger problems. But when you communicate well with your partner, you create a space where both of you feel heard, understood, and respected.

I feel more than talking effective communication is about truly listening to what your partner has to say. Often, we listen to respond rather than to understand. When your partner is sharing their thoughts, feelings or problems, it's important to be fully present and to listen carefully to what your partner is saying. Because it's important to let your partner know that their feelings matter to you and that you're there to understand their perspective. Another key part of communication is being honest and open with your partner. If something is bothering you, don't keep it inside because unspoken feelings often leads to bigger problems later. When we don't express what's on our mind, then it creates a gap between you and your partner. They will not even know something is wrong which is also unfair to them. Relationship should be big and important enough to talk about the tough things, not just the good ones.

See, it's very important to communicate with your partner even when you don't feel like talking. Often, when we're upset or hurt, our first reaction is to shut down and avoid the conversation. Because it feels easier to stay silent and we think that time will make the problem go away. But the truth is, avoiding communication actually make things worse. When you stop talking, the distance between you and your partner grows. I feel that moments when you don't want to talk are actually the times when you should talk the most. If you avoid communication during tough times, the conflict stays unresolved and may come back even bigger. However, if you face the conflict with open and honest communication, you can work through it together by talking, listening, and understanding each other's perspectives. In a relationship always express your feelings, listen to your partner, and try to find ways to work through the hard times. Remember when silence feels easier, that's when communication is most important.

Every relationship is a journey, and along the way, there are special moments that deserve to be celebrated. Recognizing and celebrating the milestones is also important aspect of growing together. Milestones, whether big or small, are reminders of the progress you've made as a couple. They can be as significant as anniversaries, date when you first met, also can be as simple as learning something new about each other, resolving a conflict, or supporting each other through a tough day. Celebrating these small moments strengthens your bond and brings joy into your relationship. It's important to take a pause in busy life and acknowledge the effort, love, and time you've invested in each other. By celebrating the milestones, you remind yourselves of how far you've come as a couple. Each milestone is a stepping stone and helping you to grow closer and understand each other more deeply. Milestones are not just about occasion itself, but about the resilience, trust, shared joy, and the willingness to grow together.

When you love someone with all your heart then one thing that you must understand is that in relationship it's not about one person winning or proving they're right in a certain situation or argument. But it's about recognizing that you and your partner are a team, and together, you can take on whatever life throws at you. When a problem comes up, big or small, it shouldn't be you vs them; it should be both of you facing the problem together. Seeing things this way makes a huge difference. Because blaming each other will not solve your problem, instead you guys should create a safe space where you can talk, listen, and find a solution as a team. Every time you do this, you're not just solving a problem but you are also strengthening your bond. You're building a relationship that will not shake easily because you know you can count on each other, no matter what.

Life is full of challenges but when you choose to stand together then every problem no matter how big it is can be solved. So, the next time when life throws a challenge, remember you're not opponents but allies. Face every obstacle together because that's how love becomes deeper and truly lasting.

As I mentioned this earlier that love is about partnership, so having shared goals and future plans is very vital aspect to have as a couples. When two people dream and work towards something together then it feels like home. Those plans and goals can be anything like saving for a house, planning travels, or even just setting goals for personal growth. By supporting each other's dreams, both big and small, you are not just building a future but building a life that has both of your hearts in it. When you plan your future with someone, you're expressing something powerful that this relationship truly matters to you, and that you see it as something meant to last. It's a way of saying, I'm not just here for today; I'm here for tomorrow, next year, and every year after that. In simple words planning a future together shows the strength of a relationship and how much it means to you. Shared goals are the foundation of commitment in relationship. So, plan your future with someone who truly deserves all you have and all you're going to become. With someone who will honour their life to you to build future together with love, respect, and loyalty. With the right person by your side, your future isn't just something to look forward to, but it's something you can start enjoying now, knowing you're building it together.

After you spend some time together we get comfortable in relationship. Over time, you get settle into daily routines, then you might start taking your partner and your relationship for granted. You get used to each other's presence, and without realizing it, you stop putting in the same effort you did in the beginning. This is why celebrating milestones are so important. These moments give you the opportunity to pause, to take step back from the routine, and appreciate one another. When you take the time to celebrate together, you remind yourself why you fell in love in the first place. By celebrating milestones and the smallest of moments, it's important to show your partner that they still matter. It's about saying, I see you, I appreciate you, and I'm grateful for everything we've built together. Because it's the moments that remind you how much you have grown together and it's important that we celebrate these moments.

As I said relationships are about teamwork, it's the journey of love and growing together means constantly learning, understanding, and supporting each other. Growing together in love means building a life that's rich with shared memories, mutual respect, and a deep understanding. When we focus on growing together, everything else tends to fall into place. Trust, respect, and love naturally increases when both people are willing to listen, support, and learn from each other.

Remember: *Where words are shared, hearts are heard, there love grows stronger. In the end, a love that grows together is a love that lasts a lifetime.*

2) Burden of Expectations

*(Expectations are like the stars we wish upon, it's far from
the reality)*

Expectations are the hopes and beliefs that we have about how things should be, especially in relationships. Expectations shape the way we think, feel, and respond to the people around us. There are some things in life that we don't have control over, no matter how hard we try and our expectations from other people are one them. Relationships are fundamental aspect of our life, providing love, support, and companionship, they enrich our experiences and contribute to our overall happiness and wellbeing. However, within the dynamics of relationships, the burden of expectations often arises. In today's self-centred world where everyone cares about what they got or what they have, and due to this selfish approach most of the peoples and relationships are facing problems around the expectations. Expectations in relationships emerge from several of sources, including societal influences, personal validations, experiences, and trying to have what others have. Expectations are simple like being loved, being priority, urge to feel special, surprises, to spend time together or some gifts. The main issue is the point at which we think about the expectations as 'Negative'. When we don't manage our expectations properly and let them control our emotions.

We all expect something in relationship or from our loved ones. Yes, we do…Only too much of expectations and its overreactions brings unhappiness and pain. When our expectations are not fulfilled, it creates a sense of unhappiness in the relationship. Expectations are the root cause of unhappiness and it's one of the main reasons why most of the relationships suffer nowadays. When one person's has some expectations and when his/her expectations are not met, it leads to frustration and a breakdown in trust resulting in emotional distance and it can erode the foundation of the relationship, leaving both humans feeling disconnected. Expectations also creates emotional stress and various issues within relationships. The fear of not meeting expectations or disappointing a partner can lead to anxiety, self-doubt, and a constant sense of pressure.

See expectations are like seeds you plant in the soil of dependency. Nurture them with your trust and understanding, but be prepared to embrace the beauty of unexpected blooms.

I) Are Expectations Real?

(Reality doesn't always match up with what we think will happen)

Alright, let's talk about expectations further. Expectations are nothing but the silent rules we set in our minds about how things should be and how people should treat us. But are our expectations real? I feel most of our expectations are not real, because if you ask yourself, then you will come to know that there is no real source of our expectations, right? The fear and expectations are created by oneself only. It cannot be created by some external force or the person.

By asking are Expectations real I am trying to say that it's very foolish of us to expect something from someone when the person from whom we are expecting is not aware of our expectations. Because we create all of our expectations in our head and the person from whom we are expecting is not even aware of our expectations. Which is very unfair for that person. It's important to understand that while expectations are a natural part of life, they're not always right. We have to be prepared for things to turn out differently than what we expect because that's what going to happen most of the time.

See life rarely turns out exactly as we expect it to. Situations change, people think differently, and circumstances evolve in unexpected ways. If we hold onto rigid expectations, we are only creating pain for ourselves. However, this does not mean we should never expect anything. Expectations become more reasonable and real when they are communicated. If the person from whom you are expecting something is aware of your thoughts, it increases the chances of your expectations being met. Even if they cannot always fulfil them, at least they have the opportunity to try. And sometimes, the act of trying itself is meaningful.

But on the other side the unspoken expectations only leads to misunderstandings and disappointment, whereas open communication fosters understanding. So instead of assuming that people will just "know" what we want, we should express our needs and desires clearly. This way, expectations become more realistic and fair. If the other person does not know about your feelings and expectations, then you are creating problem for yourself and for your partner and these expectation will only lead you to pain and disappointment.

Remember expectations are not always bad, but they must be handled with awareness. The problem arises when you expect silently, assuming others will meet your unspoken desires. But when we express our expectations, we give others the chance to understand and respond. However, even in this case, you must remain flexible, because life doesn't always go as planned.

Remember: *The more you let go of unrealistic expectations, the more peace and happiness you bring into your life.*

II) Why Do We Expect?

aving expectations is pretty normal and it's a natural part of being human. When you love, you expect. This is something our mind and the people around us tell us about expectations, and we usually don't disagree with this because we also like our expectations to get fulfilled and we also like the validation of how important we are in someone's life.

Our life is filled with expectations at every point we always tend to expect from our family, friends, from our partner and to be honest most of us fails to control these expectations most of the times. Sometimes it's very fair to expect, but most of the time, expectations are created by our own hopes and desires. Which may not match with the reality and due to this we create mess in our lives.

So let me start with the simple question have you really asked yourself why do you expect? Why you have this expectation at this moment? No right?

We often expect something from someone but we never ask ourselves why do we expect? Let me tell you why we expect and there are so many reasons behind our expectations. It depends on the individual, on his/her emotions and feelings that he/she carries inside. Most of us expect out of love when we love someone, we expect certain behaviour of that person towards us, we expect that person should live like this which is sometimes right, because we don't want that person to go through failures and pain like us. These expectations come from our own experiences we have seen pain, faced failures, and struggled through hardships. And because we care deeply, we don't want our loved one to go through the same difficulties. We want the best for them, a life free from unnecessary struggles. We believe that if they make the right choices, they can avoid the mistakes we once made. It's our way of protecting them, of ensuring their happiness.

But this is not why we expect every time right? Sometimes we expect them to behave according to ourselves because of our need and selfish behaviour. We want that person to be like us because deep down we all consider ourselves right in every situation, we also consider that I am the best person in this world and we want everyone to be like us. But it's important to understand that everyone thinks like that, nobody likes to be wrong. The one most important thing we must understand is that everyone is hero in their own lives, it's just matter of perspective.

Another reason why most of us expect is because of our own need of validation, from own need of validation I am trying to say that, we often need validations from others that we are important, that we are enough for them and only our existence should matter to them. Let's take this example on your friend's birthday you had gave him a nice surprise so on your birthday you will expect him to do the same for you, you will need that validation that I am also important and a priority in my friends life. Expectations are directly proportional to the magnitude of the efforts that we put in for someone. We don't expect from a random person, from the people we don't know because we haven't put any efforts for them.

Expectations also arise when you have trust on people. If you trust someone you expect them to behave in a certain way, we expect them to stay in our life forever, to not break our heart. We might expect them to support us during tough times, share our joys, and be honest with us. We look for them to understand our feelings without us having to explain everything. Trust makes us believe that they will keep their promises and stand by us no matter what happens. With our building trust on someone, the expectations also increase from that person. For example If a boss trusts his employee then he will expect that the employee will complete the task without his supervision, which may lead to the failure of task. This is where the fine balance between trust and oversight becomes important. Trust is a beautiful thing, it builds strong connections and encourages growth. But blind trust, without communication or accountability, can lead to disappointment and regret.

Another reason why we expect from others is that we think we always do well for others. We've always done things for others and have always been there for them. When we have this thinking in our mind that we've done so many things for others, it's very natural to expect the same in return. We might feel that our kindness and support should be acknowledged and reciprocated. This expectation is rooted in the belief that relationships are a two-way street, where mutual effort and care are essential. We anticipate that others will offer us the same loyalty, help, and understanding that we have given them. When we invest time, energy, and emotions into someone, we hope they value and respect our contributions, leading us to expect similar treatment in return.

Remember: *Even good things can become bad if taken to excess Expectations can be normal part of life but excess of expectations will only lead you to misery. Be the one who manages expectations and don't give them power to ruin your life and relationships.*

III) Setting the Right Expectations

(Love lasts when expectations are based on reality, not fantasy.)

Relationships thrive on mutual understanding, respect, and love, but they can falter under the weight of unrealistic expectations. When it comes to a healthy relationships, having the right expectations is important for building a healthy and fulfilling connection. It's natural to want your partner to fulfil certain needs and dreams, but problems arises when those expectations become wrong and unfair. This section is about, what it means to have right expectations or what are right expectations and how this approach strengthens bond between two people.

Now first things first, when we love someone, we naturally want the best for them. In every relationship, there comes a time when you notice something about your partner a habit, a behaviour which can cause problem in their life, or even a mind-set that you believe isn't right. And you want them to change that certain behaviour or a habit then it's a right expectation. Because you are wanting the best for your partner and it shows that you care about their growth and well-being. I feel in relationships, change is not just inevitable but it's also essential.

Many people believe that changing yourself in a relationship is a negative thing that it means losing your identity or giving up who you are. But in reality changing yourself in a relationship is a sign of maturity and love. It shows that you care enough to make an effort for the other person. Change isn't always easy. It takes effort, self-awareness, and sometimes even a little discomfort. You might feel resistant at first, thinking, "Why should I change? This is who I am." And that's fair. But relationships aren't about standing still; they're about moving forward together. When both people are willing to adapt and evolve, the relationship becomes a partnership built on mutual respect and understanding. Change in a relationship is about creating a better version of your shared life together. It's about making the effort to understand each other, compromise when needed, and grow as individuals while building something beautiful as a couple.

So wanting your partner's behaviour or habits to change isn't about trying to control them but it's about wanting a life which is best for them and also that's fulfilling and meaningful for both of you. When approached with love, patience, and understanding, then this kind of expectation can be not only right but also fulfilling for both your partner and the bond you share.

Striking the right balance in what you expect from your partner is key for maintaining a healthy and fulfilling relationship. Wanting your partner to have a job is a reasonable expectation.

It reflects a desire for their stability, responsibility, and growth. However, wanting your partner to be rich veers into the territory of unrealistic and wrong expectations. Another example I can tell you is like expecting your partner to communicate openly is fair, but expecting them to never disagree with you is unrealistic. Hoping for your partner to be supportive is reasonable, but demanding that they solve all your problems is unfair.

See In the journey of love, setting the right expectations is like choosing the right path. It doesn't mean giving up on your dreams or lowering your standards. Instead, it's about being realistic, understanding, and compassionate. Having right expectations allows you to build a relationship that is grounded in reality and enriched by mutual efforts. It helps you appreciate your partner for who they are, rather than who you think they should be. By setting your expectations right, you pave the way for a relationship that can weather challenges, celebrate triumphs, and grow stronger with time.

Remember: *Having expectations is normal, but having the right expectations is what makes a relationship thrive. So set them wisely, and watch your love flourish.*

IV) Letting Go of Expectations

(The best part of expectations is you can always lower them)

Now we know that having too much on expectations can lead to disappointments and frustration when things don't go as planned. If you see in life what matters the most is to take control of our life because most of the time we are not in control of what we are doing and expectations is one of that thing. Letting go of expectations doesn't mean giving up on what we want or deserve; it means freeing ourselves from relying on others for our happiness. It's about taking control of our own lives and finding joy within ourselves. By letting go of our expectations, we open ourselves to new possibilities and a greater peace. It's not easy to let go of all your expectations. So instead of trying to eliminate expectations completely, the real lesson is to learn how to manage them and lower them where necessary.

The first and most essentials thing to do when you want to let go of your expectations is to set boundaries. Setting boundaries is like building strong walls around our feelings. It might seem hard, but it's important to protect ourselves. We need to know what's okay and what's not, while still being open to growing together. Having boundaries also helps you to keep your own identity in a relationship. Even though you're with someone, you still have your own feelings, opinions, and things you like to do. When these boundaries are respected, it helps build trust between two people. While setting boundaries you tell the other people's what you're okay with and what you're not, it stops them from doing the things that might hurt you or make you feel bad. In life, it's important not to let anyone have too much power over you. When someone has too much control and power over you they can make you feel really bad and can make you miserable. That's why setting boundaries is super important. No matter how someone treats you, you should be happy within yourself and should not get affected by anyone's behaviour. So when you set healthy limits on what you accept from others, you stop depending on them to fulfil your expectations. You learn to give yourself the love, respect, and validation you once sought from others.

The truth of life is nobody is perfect, nobody really is, not you, your partner and not even your role model or the person you admire most. Everyone makes mistakes, that's why pencils have erasers. Making mistakes is part of being human. When someone does not live up to your expectations, hurt you, make you feel bad then try walking in their shoes. It's the best way to see the world from a different perspective. Like, if you're always looking at a painting from one side, but when you move that painting and see it from a different angle, it might look totally different. That's what it feels like when you try to understand how someone else feels or thinks. It helps you see the world in a whole new way, and it can make you more understanding and kind. When you begin to care about how other people feel, you can change what you expect from them. It's all about understanding what others can and can't do.

Each of us has unique flaws inside us. We all have things we're not so good at but doesn't everyone deserves to be happy? Accepting each other's flaws and strengths makes any relationships stronger. As I said in relationship, growth and change are necessary. You will evolve, adjust, and make changes because love requires effort. But at the same time, it's also important to understand that some things about your partner will never change and that's okay. We are all different and you cannot expect your partner to be everything you want them to be all the time. Love is not about finding a perfect person, it's about loving an imperfect person perfectly. Like in puzzle each piece is different, some are little, and some are big. But when they all fit together, it creates a beautiful picture. That's like accepting each other's flaws and strengths. We might not be perfect, but together, we make something wonderful. It shows that we all deserve love and respect, even with our imperfections.

Life is not a play or a movie and life simply doesn't follow our script. Instead, life is like a rollercoaster, with twists and turns we don't always see coming. Sometimes we expect things to happen in a certain way but that's not how life will turn out every time. When things go wrong, we often blame others or the situation. But have you ever thought about changing yourself instead? Isn't that just as important? It's like when we're playing a game and we keep losing. Instead of blaming the game or others, maybe we should just practice more or try a different strategy. May be the fault lies in us that we are not able to see. See life may not follow the script but we should be able to rewrite the story, to adjust our sails when the wind changes its direction. Being able to change and adapt helps us to deal with life's ups and downs. It's all about being flexible and adjusting our expectations when things don't go as planned.

Only you truly understand yourself and your intentions. You don't always have to prove yourself to others. Trust your own feelings and motives. Sometimes, it's enough to know your own worth without seeking validation from others. In a world that's always changing, it's important to keep your eyes on your own dreams and desires. Your happiness and well-being should be your top priority. Instead of relying and always expecting from others, invest in yourself because you are your biggest asset. Don't waste time waiting for validation or expecting too much from others. Trust yourself, believe in your abilities, and keep moving forward towards your goals. Surround yourself with supportive people who lift you up, not who lets you down. When face any setbacks, see that setback as opportunity to learn and grow. Celebrate your achievements, no matter how small they are, and give yourself credit for your hard work. You're in control and driver of your own journey, so make it a fulfilling one.

At last Every one, I repeat everyone no matter how close you are with someone, no matter how much they love you or you love them, will let you down at some point in life, it's inevitable and you will do the same and will let down others too. So it's not right to put the burden of your expectations on someone else as nobody will ever be able to fulfil your every need, they can never be able to stand on each of your expectation. If you expect nothing from somebody you will never be disappointed and ideally when we truly love someone then the problem with expectations should not arrive as god made everybody different. We should give everything that we can give in any relationship and to the person that we love that's the best and purest way of loving someone. If you lower your expectations, the argument goes, then you won't be disappointed. Don't let your momentarily expectations, ruin your relationship.

Remember: *Turn your focus inward, rather than outward. Accept the things the way they are instead of fighting them, if we practice gratitude instead of always wanting more and if we recognize that the only person we can control is ourselves, a life of no expectations, no disappointments will follow.*

3) Heartbreak

We all know that love is one of the most beautiful experiences in life. It fills our hearts with joy, makes us feel alive, and gives us a sense of belonging. We celebrate love, cherish it, and dream about it. We focus and talk so much about love that in all this, we often forget an important truth, that heartbreak is also a part of love.

We rarely talk about heartbreak, it's something almost everyone experiences at some point in their life. We focus so much on finding love, keeping love, and nurturing love that we ignore the possibility of loss. What happens when the person we love leaves us? When a relationship ends suddenly, when promises are broken, or when the future we imagined disappears in an instant? Heartbreak is painful. It shakes us, changes us, and sometimes makes us question everything. But just like love, heartbreak has its own lessons to teach. It's not the end of the story, it's just a chapter of growth, healing, and self-discovery.

In this section, I will talk about heartbreak not as something to fear, but as something to understand. How do we deal with the pain? How do we heal? And most importantly, how do we move forward when someone we love is no longer by our side?

I) Those Who Left You Never Loved You

(Don't cry for those who left you, their absence just made space for someone who will truly love you.)

What I'm about to share or tell you might be a bit of hard to take in, but sometimes, we have to face reality, no matter how challenging it may be. Most of the times in life we avoid and ignore the truth because truth feels uncomfortable and even painful. Reality isn't always what we want it to be but we have to face it and be honest with ourselves about it. In this section, we'll look at the importance of acknowledging things as they are, without any filters or wishful thinking. I understand that when someone walks out of your life, it can be one of the most painful experiences. The end of any relationship whether it's a friendship, a romantic relationship, or even family ties, can leave us feeling heartbroken, confused, and wondering why it happened. But sometimes, the truth is that those who left may not have truly loved you, at least not in the way that genuine love is meant to last.

Look around you. The people surrounding you aren't just faces in your life; they're part of your story. You have memories with them, both joyful and challenging. You've laughed with them, shared countless good times, and also gone through moments when you couldn't stand each other. You've argued, fought, and maybe even swore you'd never talk to them again. Yet, here you are, still together. Why? Because you love them and they love you and love doesn't just walk away when things get tough. Real relationships are built on resilience. They're about forgiving, growing, and choosing each other even when it's hard. You've stayed because, deep down, you care. Love and loyalty run deeper than any argument. Basically I want you to know that you don't give up on people who really mean something to you, and you mean something to them. People who have been with you through laughter and tears, through misunderstandings and forgiveness. This not giving up attitude what makes your bond strong. Life is not just about the easy times but about sticking together through everything.

Now you are left by someone you loved deeply. They broke your heart into pieces, and the pain feels unbearable. It's hard to accept, isn't it? After all, you gave them your heart, your time, your love, everything that you had. But as difficult as it is to believe, they've made it clear. They no longer love you, or perhaps they lost the love they once had for you. And that's the truth they just don't love you anymore and there is nothing beyond this. Yes, it hurts. It feels like the world has crumbled beneath your feet. Every breath feels heavier, every moment is lonelier, and it's hard to face the reality staring back at you. But no matter how painful it is, the truth is if they left you they never loved you. If they had truly loved you, they would have stayed. Love doesn't walk away when things get hard, love fights, it stays, and it grows through the challenges. True love doesn't abandon you in the storm; it stands beside you, holding your hand. But the ones who left? They didn't love you the way you deserve to be loved. Maybe they cared, maybe they felt something for you once, but it wasn't enough. Not enough to stay, not enough to choose you, not enough to fight for what you both had.

And as harsh as that truth may be, it's also liberating. Because now you know they weren't your forever. They weren't the person who was meant to hold your heart for a lifetime. And that's okay. It doesn't make their leaving hurt any less, but it does mean you can stop chasing them in your mind, stop wondering what you could have done differently. Because love, real love, wouldn't have let you question your worth. Real love wouldn't have let you feel so alone. The people who leave you aren't meant to stay, no matter how much you wish they would. I know relationships are tough. They feel like walking through a storm, with challenges coming at you from every direction. It's hard not to give up when things get tough. When misunderstandings grow, when words hurt, when life itself tests the strength of your bond, it can feel easier to let go than to keep holding on. There are always a thousand reasons to leave….

But amongst those thousand reasons, there is one reason to stay. And that reason is love.

Yes, I know love doesn't make the hard times disappear, but it gives you the strength to fight through them. It gives you patience when tempers run high. It gives you understanding when words fail. It gives you hope when everything feels like it's falling apart. Love reminds you that relationships aren't perfect, but they are worth fighting for. Love is a choice. Every day, you have to choose to stay, to fight, and to nurture what you've built over the time. It's not always easy but it's important because you love them.

To be honest love is not always easy. We may not have the perfect story that we see in movies, where everything falls into place without effort. Real love requires work, patience, and understanding. Love is path filled with learning, growth, and understanding. In love you always have to make sacrifices for the person you love and it's not only about sacrifices. It's also about constant efforts. Falling in love is effortless. It happens naturally sometimes in an instant, sometimes over time. But to make your love last, it requires constant efforts, relationships need constant care to stay strong. You also have to let go of mistakes because forgiveness is also an act of love. No one is perfect, and mistakes will happen. So the right person the one who truly loves you will do all of this willingly. They won't see sacrifices, effort, or forgiveness as burdens. Instead, they'll see them as opportunities to strengthen your bond. They'll want to fight for you, with you and for your relationship because they know it's worth it. They'll find happiness in making you feel loved, supported, and understood. Remember love is not about finding someone who makes everything easy; it's about finding someone who makes everything worthwhile. It's about being with a person who chooses you, every single day, no matter how hard things get.

See, it's very easy to give up when things get hard. When a relationship hits a rough patch, when misunderstandings pile up, and when emotions run high. But it's very tough to hold on and the right person won't give up just because it's hard. They won't let a temporary storm destroy what you've built together. The right person will hold on. They'll choose you, even on the days when you feel unlovable. They'll make adjustments not because they're forced to, but because they want to. They'll understand that love is about compromise, about meeting each other halfway, and about finding solutions instead of focusing on problems. When someone truly loves you, they won't leave you heartbroken. They won't let you carry the weight of the relationship alone. Instead, they'll stand beside you, ready to share the burden. But if someone walks away, when they leave when times get tough or they refuse to make an effort then it's a painful sign that they may not love you the way you deserve to be loved. True love doesn't abandon. It doesn't give up when the road gets rough. If someone leaves, it's not because you weren't enough; it's because they weren't the right person for you. You deserve a love that holds on. A love that fights for you, for the relationship, and for the future you're building together.

Remember: *You deserve someone who chooses to stay, who chooses you, every single day. Right person wouldn't leave. They wouldn't let you suffer alone. The right person would stay, work through the challenges because at its core love isn't just about the good times, it's about holding on through the hard ones, too. And people do say that it's real when it comes back but for me it's real when they never left.*

II) There is Always a 1% Chance

(Loving someone means accepting the risk that one day, they may walk away.)

In life, we often think that once we find the right person, everything will be perfect forever. We picture a future together, filled with love, happiness, and shared dreams. And sometimes, it feels like we've found that one person who is meant to be with us, who makes everything better. But here's a hard truth, no matter how great things seem, there is always a chance, no matter how small that your partner might leave you.

It's something that nobody wants to think about or talk about, especially when you're in a loving relationship. Because when we are in love, we often see only what we want to see. We focus on the beautiful moments, the deep emotions, and the happiness our partner brings us. We hold on to the good times so tightly that we ignore the uncomfortable truths that may be right in front of us. Love has a way of making us blind to reality. Instead of looking at the facts, we give more importance to our emotions. We overlook red flags, make excuses for hurtful behavior, and convince ourselves that everything is fine even when it's not. Sometimes, we choose to believe in potential rather than reality, hoping that things will change instead of accepting them as they are.

But true love is not just about feelings; it's also about clarity. And the reality is, life is unpredictable. People change. Circumstances change. We change. And sometimes, even though we try our best, things don't work out the way we hoped. 1% seem small but it's real. It's the possibility that, no matter how perfect your relationship feels right now, there's a tiny chance that something could go wrong. When I am talking about that 1% I am not being negative I just want you to acknowledge that life isn't always in our control, and love isn't always guaranteed. Yes, it's important to stay hopeful and to appreciate the good things in our relationships. But it's also important to recognize that there is a possibility of loss and when we do that we will be at least ready for the challenges that can come our way.

See every relationship, comes with a degree of unpredictability. Life is filled with uncertainty human emotions circumstances are ever changing and when two people come together, they bring their own unique set of experiences, emotions, and expectations. Emotions are the heart of any relationship. But emotions are also fluid. They aren't static and they don't always stay the same. One day, you might feel incredibly connected and in tune with your partner, the next, you might find yourselves facing misunderstandings and frustrations. And this emotions and feelings also changes based on so many factors like stress at work, personal insecurities, a loss of a loved one, or even just the everyday challenges that life throws at us. And due to this relationship can suffer and this doesn't mean the love isn't real, but emotions are complicated and can change the dynamics of the relationship.

People too, are constantly changing. We grow, we evolve, and sometimes we change in ways that are hard to predict. A person you met years ago may not be the same person today, and that's true for both you and your partner. We go through experiences that shape us in different ways, and that can affect how we view the world, and how we connect with others. And these changes can also affect the relationship. Two people who were once perfect for each other and were flawlessly aligned in their goals, dreams, and values might start to feel like they are growing apart over time. The one thing that you must understand that we are all different humans and our journeys are also different and will not always follow the same path.

I feel the idea of complete certainty in relationships is an illusion. It's true that some relationships flourish and stay strong over the time, but not all relationships work out the way we hope. When we are in a relationship, we naturally want it to succeed. But as there is always a possibility of heartbreak and it's important to acknowledge this uncertainty, by preparing ourselves mentally for the possibility of this heartbreak. This preparation doesn't mean expecting a failure or living in fear, but rather, accepting that life may take us down to an unexpected paths. By preparing mentally, you don't have to lessen the love you have or the importance of the relationship. This mental preparation means preparing yourself to be stronger and better emotionally to deal with anything life might throw at you. It's about being prepared for all the eventualities and making yourself emotionally stronger. And when heartbreak does come, as difficult as it may be, we will be mentally prepared. Heartbreak is never easy, but when we're prepared for the possibility of things might not always work out, then we are less likely to feel completely lost or crushed by the situation. Instead, we will be able to face the sadness with more clarity and strength.

In relationships, most of the people give everything that they have, their time, efforts, and emotions. But what happens when in a relationship we lose ourselves and the relationship becomes everything in our life? When our identity becomes so entangled with someone else that we lose sight of who we are? That tiny 1% chance it's also a gentle reminder that never lose yourself in a relationship. When we give too much of ourselves to someone else, we risk forgetting the unique individual we are. We tend to ignore our own dreams, hobbies, and passions because our world revolves around the relationship. But is this fair to you?

Your individual identity matters. It's what makes you you. It's the reason your partner was drawn to you in the first place. Focus on your personal growth, because when you do that you bring more to the table in the relationship. You bring confidence, energy, and a sense of fulfilment that comes from living a life true to yourself. I do feel that relationships can and should be a big part of your life, but they shouldn't be all of your life. Pursue your passions. Set personal goals. Nurture your friendships. Spend time with yourself and your family. Because that is also a large part of your life. So, remember a great relationship doesn't erase who you are it just enhances it. Always focus on yourself, give the love that you give to your partner to your family and friends also. Because often, it's you, your family, and your friends who help you heal, who remind you of your worth, and who give you the love you need to move forward. Don't make the mistake of giving so much to one relationship that you lose touch with the other parts of your life. A healthy balance is essential. Give your heart to those who deserve it not just to the one person, but also to yourself, to your family, and to your friends.

Love is one of the most beautiful feelings in the world. It's powerful, transformative, and fills our life with meaning. But in the midst of this beauty in of love, always hold a small part of yourself back. This doesn't mean loving less or being distant. It means loving with a sense of self awareness and balance. No matter how much you love someone, it's vital to remember that 1%. By holding yourself back just a little, you create space where you can love without losing yourself.

So love without any attachments, cherish the present without clinging to expectations or the past. Enjoy the beauty of the relationship for what it is right now, rather than always thinking about the future. When you love without attachment, you're not holding back your emotions but you're protecting your inner peace. This balance will only strengthen your relationship. Laugh together, grow together, and build memories. But at the same time, hold on to the person that you are outside of the relationship. Keep pursuing your own passions, and maintain the relationships that enrich your life. So, love deeply, but don't lose yourself. Be in present, but not overly attached.

Remember: *The paradox of 1% may seem small but its possibility and reality that in life NOTHING IS GUARANTEED!!*

III) The Art of Letting Go

(Some chapters in life must end for new ones to begin.)

Losing someone you love and being heartbroken it's one of the toughest phases that you will ever go through in life. In those moments, the world feels like it's spinning off its axis. Everything seems unreal, like you're caught in a dream you can't wake up from. The pain wraps around you, heavy and unrelenting, making even the simplest things feel impossible. And here's where we all make a mistake. We get stuck in an endless cycle of thoughts, replaying every moment, every word, every "what if" in our minds. We hold onto the pain as if it's the only thing left of what we lost. And, we even bury ourselves in that pain, which consumes our days and nights. And nothing is worth that much & nothing good will ever come out of that. If you find yourself trapped in such a cycle of pain and self-destruction, it's a sign that it's time to let go.

See letting go of someone you love is one of the hardest things you'll ever have to do in life. It's like trying to loosen your grip on something your heart desperately wants to hold onto. But the truth is, holding on hurts more than letting go ever will. Let me put it this way, love doesn't disappear just because the relationship has ended. That love stays with you. It becomes a part of your story. Letting go isn't about forgetting the person you loved or pretending the feelings weren't real. It's not about erasing the memories or denying the impact they had on your life. Those moments were real, and so was the love that you shared. Letting go doesn't mean you have to speak badly about them or diminish what they meant to you. No letting go has bigger and deeper meaning than this, it's about accepting that things have changed and holding onto the past will only hurt you.

Love, even when it ends, deserves respect. Just because the relationship didn't last doesn't mean the love wasn't meaningful or true. Breakup doesn't make the person you love villain of your story. Letting go means you have to release the emotional attachment that's holding you back so you can find peace within yourself. Think of it like setting a bird free from a cage. You're not denying the bird's beauty or the joy it brought you. You're simply allowing it to fly. Another thing you should keep in mind is that releasing any emotional attachment is a process, and it doesn't happen overnight. It requires patience and kindness towards yourself. There will be days when memories will hit you, or pain will feel fresh again. And that's okay. Healing isn't a straight line; it's a journey. As you release the attachment, you'll start to feel lighter. Eventually memories will stop stinging, and the pain will also feel lighter. The first step or the most important thing to do after the heartbreak is to release the emotional attachment and to make a space for yourself, for your healing, and for the new beginnings that await you.

When you are heartbroken, then you become more fragile, more emotional, and more vulnerable person. As if your heart is wide open and exposed to every little thing. And yes, this phase is incredibly tough. You will find yourself crying at unexpected moments or overwhelmed by the smallest memories. It feels like your emotions are running all over you no matter how hard you try, you can't seem to control them. But here's an important thing you must keep in mind, is that it's completely okay to feel emotional, after all you're a human but letting your emotions completely take over you will only make your journey of letting go harder. It's like pouring water into a cup that's already overflowing. I feel true letting go is almost emotionless process. It's not about dramatic goodbyes or overwhelming pain. It's about reaching to a point where you no longer allow your emotions to dictate your actions. So it's important to not let your emotions control you. Because when it comes to letting go and moving on emotions can cloud your judgment and even makes it harder to make the right decision. So having emotions is good, but don't let them take control of you.

In heartbreak the sadness is very heavy, the pain is sharp, and the world seems a darker place. Because of this we make mistake of resisting our feelings. You tell yourself, I shouldn't feel this way, or I need to be strong and move on. But here's the thing: the more you resist your emotions or feelings the more they persist. See resisting your emotions doesn't make them disappear. Feelings are like waves they rise, they peak, and they fall.

So don't try to push them away or ignore them that makes you get engaged in them. You must give your emotions the space to exist so they can eventually fade on their own. Remind yourself that it's okay to feel this way. Don't judge yourself for being emotional, it's just a sign that you cared deeply. Give yourself permission to cry because emotions also need to flow to be released. Heartbreak feels like the end of the world, but it's not it's just a chapter in your story. Life is a book with many pages, and no single chapter defines the entire story. Just because this chapter is filled with pain doesn't mean the next one won't be filled with joy, growth, and love. Every great story has moments of struggle, moments when the protagonist feels lost or defeated. But those moments are what make the victories so meaningful.

The truth is letting go is a hard thing to do, but sometimes, it's the only way to find peace. And the hardest reality I can tell you is that anything that feels forced or constantly brings you pain is not meant for you. Love is not supposed to be a battle where you lose yourself in the process. You might say that "I loved them. I wanted it to work." It's normal to want something to last when you've given your heart to it. But love should never feel like you're forcing something that doesn't fit anymore, right? If it's causing you more pain than joy, then this is not what you truly deserve. The right things in life will never require you to force them, and the right love will feel like home not a battlefield. Imagine like this you are carrying a heavy backpack filled with stones. Each stone represents a memory, a grudge, or a pain caused by the person who broke your heart. And the weight of this backpack slows you down, drains your energy, and keeps you from enjoying the journey of life. Would you continue to carry it? No right? Ask yourself the person who broke your heart, made you miserable does that person, still deserve your energy? Holding onto past or that person is like watering a dead plant. No matter how much effort you put into it, the plant will never bloom again. Holding on to your past will ruin your present moment and possibly the future as well. Holding on to the past is never worth it, so let go and reclaim your energy.

To let go of the person who broke your heart, one thing that you must understand that, everything is not within your control. The world is unpredictable. People, situations, and their opinions often change without warning. However what you can control, is your reaction towards it. See the truth is you can't control what others say or do. You can't force someone to stay, to love you, or to treat you right. But you can decide how you'll respond. Forget everything they said or did to you when they walked away it does not define who you are. Do not let their actions define your happiness. Carrying resentment or pain doesn't punish the person who hurt you, it punishes you. You have a choice, don't let someone's actions to take space in your heart and mind. The pain you are going through might not be your fault, but healing or what's coming over is your responsibility. You are stronger than the hurt, wiser than the pain, so don't let someone else's mistakes steal your joy. Remember, the person who broke your heart doesn't have power over you unless you give it to them. The world may be beyond your control, but your peace is always in your hands.

When someone fails to love you the way you deserve or treats you badly, it's easy to blame yourself. You start wondering, Was it something I said? Was I not good enough? But let me tell you something important their behaviour is not your fault. It's their problem, not yours. Because how someone treats you says more about them than it does about you. Their actions reflect their personality, insecurities, or inability to value the goodness in front of them. So don't let their shortcomings make you question your worth.

If someone fails to see your value, does that make you any less of a good person? Of course not. Their inability to recognize your worth doesn't define you. You don't have to shrink yourself to fit into someone else's limited perspective of love or respect. See you are not responsible for someone else's behaviour. People make their own choices, and how they act is a reflection of their inner world. You could give them all the love, kindness, and effort in the world, and still they can treat you poorly and that's on them. So don't be hard on yourself. Don't let one person's actions make you question your value. You deserve the love that lifts you up, respects you, and celebrates you. Anything less than that isn't worth your time or energy. You deserve the world, and deep down, you know it. Life is too short to waste on people who don't see your light. The love you truly deserve is out there somewhere. But to find that, you have to starts with you. Love yourself enough to walk away from anyone who doesn't treat you the way you deserve. Because you are worth it.

Acceptance is the key to letting go. The moment you stop fighting what is and start embracing it for what it truly is you make progress. This doesn't mean you have to like or agree with the situations. Acceptance simply means saying, this is what happened, and I can't change it or the past. It's about facing the truth with courage, without denying or resisting it. When you cling to the "if's" and "but's" you keep yourself trapped in a cycle of pain. See the reality never change. But this clinging does change your ability to move forward. The path of moving forward only starts with acceptance. Acceptance is that act of letting go. See you may never fully understand why something happened. So Instead of seeking answers, focus on seeking peace and moving forward. Suffering only comes when you cling to something that no longer serves you. Free yourself from the weight of what you can't control to find a sense of relief, a sense of freedom. Every time you choose to accept what is, rather than fight against it, you grow stronger. Acceptance is the bridge that takes you from pain to peace. Remember Happiness isn't found in wishing the past were different. It's found in accepting the present and trusting that better days are ahead.

Letting go isn't just about moving on from the past, the important step in letting go is to forgive the person who hurt you, and more importantly, you must forgive yourself. Forgiveness is for you. It's about releasing the anger, and pain that tie you to the past. The universe has its way of balancing things out. When someone causes pain, that energy doesn't just disappear. It comes back to them in ways you may never see or expect. Trust that life has a way of teaching everyone the lessons they need, in its own time. What I am trying to say is karma will take care of the person who treated you horribly. You must forgive yourself. Don't blame yourself for trusting the wrong person, for not seeing the red flags, or for staying too long in a hurtful situation. You are human and we all make mistakes. You made choices based on what you knew and felt at the time. Forgive yourself, let go, and trust that the universe has your back.

At the end of the day, life is about learning to let go. It's one of the hardest lessons, but also one of the most important. As much as we try to hold onto people, moments, or even things, there comes a time when we must say goodbye. That's the reality of life that everything is temporary. Once you truly understand this, it will change the way you live. Letting go means accepting the natural flow of life. Life is a journey, not a permanent stop. People will come and go, situations will change, and time never stands still. Everything is temporary, learn to see beauty in the fleeting nature of life. Every chapter, every person, and every moment plays a role in shaping who we are. At the end of our lives, we have to say goodbye to everything and everyone. It's not a punishment, it's the natural cycle of life. Knowing that everything is temporary reminds us to love deeply, live fully, and cherish every moment. Instead of fearing goodbyes, learn to see them as transitions.

The art of letting go is about trust. Trust that life knows what it's doing. Trust that every loss has a lesson. So, let go the person you once loved the most, let go of the past that holds you back. Let go of the fear of the unknown. Let go of the need to control what's beyond your reach. Trust the flow of life, and you'll find a peace that no attachment can bring. In the end, the only thing you truly own is the love you give and the memories you create.

Remember: *Letting go isn't the end, it's the beginning of freedom, peace, and a life well-lived.*

IV) There is Always a Light at the End of the Tunnel

(The darkness may slow you down, but it can never stop you from reaching the light.)

Heartbreak feels like walking through a dark, endless tunnel with no map and no sign of where it ends. The pain is overwhelming, making every step forward feel like a battle. You feel like the hurt will last forever. But here's the truth about tunnels, they always lead somewhere. There's light waiting, even if you can't see it right now. This chapter is a reminder that healing is not only possible but inevitable. The journey through heartbreak may feel endless, but there is light waiting for you at the end of the tunnel. It's a gentle promise that the weight you carry today will become lighter, that the cracks in your heart will make room for something beautiful. In the darkest moments, it's hard to believe that the light will return, but every story of healing begins in this very darkness and in this journey through healing, you'll find strength you didn't know you had, clarity you didn't expect, and a new version of yourself that's ready for a brighter tomorrow.

Now the first and probably the most important thing you all must understand that PAIN NEVER LASTS FOREVER. In fact, nothing in life is permanent not the joy, not the sorrow, not even the challenges we face. Just like the night makes way for the morning, the darkest moments of your life will eventually pass. Life is always moving forward, always changing, and with every ending comes the possibility of a fresh start. The pain and heartbreak will not last forever as well. See in every ending there is a chance for a new beginning. Its nature's way of showing us that when a door closes, a window opens, offering us new opportunities to grow, heal, and rediscover joy. The key is to focus on the positives, even when they feel hard to see. Staying positive doesn't mean ignoring the pain or pretending it doesn't exist. It means choosing to believe that better days are ahead. It's about holding on to hope. Life is full of windows that are open, but we must choose to see them. They may not be where we expect, and they may require effort to reach, but they are there, offering hope and renewal. So when any relationship ends in your life remind yourself that endings aren't final. They're transitions. They're reminders to look for the window, for the opportunity, for the fresh beginning that's waiting just around the corner. Trust the life, god, journey, and keep moving forward.

I know what it feels like to be broken. I've been there. There were days when I didn't want to live anymore. Days when everything felt pointless, and the pain was so overwhelming that it seemed easier to just give up. I wanted to escape-escape my feelings, my family, my own mind. I remember my body trembling, my hands shaking as I sat there, unable to find peace or strength.

But if there's one thing I've learned through all of it, it's this: nothing heals a broken heart better than time. When you're in the middle of heartbreak, it feels like the world has stopped. Every moment is heavy, and every breath is a reminder of what you've lost. People will tell you to "stay strong" or "move on," but those words feel hollow when your heart is shattered. It's hard to believe that the pain will ever go away.

I know how tempting it is to run away from your emotions, from the people who love you and even from yourself. You just want to forget everything, to turn off the noise in your head. But here's the thing: running away doesn't heal you. It just pushes the pain to the side, and sooner or later, it comes back even stronger. Healing isn't easy. It doesn't happen overnight. There's no magic switch that makes the pain disappear. See time will not erase your memories, but it will soften the edges of your pain. The nights where you cry yourself to sleep. One day, they'll become fewer and farther between. The ache that feels like it's carved into your chest. It will fade, little by little. Time has this quiet, invisible way of mending what feels unfixable.

And one day, you'll wake up, and the heaviness in your chest won't feel as suffocating, and without realizing you will feel lighter.

So if you're reading this and you're in that dark place, I want you to hold on. It might not feel like it right now, but things will get better. Take it one moment at a time. Let time do its work. Be patient with yourself, even when it feels impossible.

You will laugh again. You will love again. And when that day comes, you'll look back at this chapter of your life and see how far you've come. You'll realize that the broken pieces of your heart have healed, not perfectly, but beautifully. And in that moment, you'll know: you made it. So hang in there, take a deep breath, and remind yourself, my time will come and it will definitely come.

When you're going through heartbreak, it feels like every moment drags on, heavy with sadness and thoughts you can't escape. But let me tell you something this is not how it's always going to be. Life has a way of surprising us. The same way joy doesn't last forever, pain doesn't either. Life is always changing its never constant. The good times, the bad times, the heartbreaks, and the victories they all come and go. Feelings are powerful, aren't they? When something good happens, we feel like we're on top of the world. When something bad happens, it feels like the world is crashing down around us. Don't attach yourself too closely to the emotions you feel. Whether they're good or bad, they're just passing through, like clouds in the sky. Life is full of ups and downs, so instead of riding every high and sinking with every low, try to find stillness within yourself. Don't let any feelings control you. Find balance in every situation of life because good things aren't as good as you think and bad things aren't as bad as they seem.

Now imagine standing on the shore, watching the waves. Some waves are big and powerful, others are small and gentle. But no matter what, the waves keep coming and going. Your feelings are just like those waves. They rise, they fall, and then they're gone. If you attach yourself to every wave, you'll feel like you're being tossed around by the ocean. But if you stay grounded and still, you can watch the waves without letting them control you.

I feel life is never as simple as "good" or "bad." It's a mix of everything, constantly changing. When you learn to stay still calm and grounded you'll realize that you don't have to be swept away by every feeling. So the next time you feel overwhelmed whether by joy or sorrow remind yourself: this is just a moment, not the whole story. Stay still. Stay present. Because no matter what you do life will always keep moving forward.

Now, another thing that you should keep in mind is that in the journey it's not only about reaching at the end of the tunnel. It's about becoming the better version of yourself on the other side of the tunnel.

Heartbreak. It's a word that carries so much weight inside it. The pain, the emptiness, the feeling that your world has been flipped upside down. When you're in it, it feels like the end. And all of this is true, but beyond this heartbreak also is something else. Heartbreak is a teacher, the kind that doesn't whisper lessons gently but engraves them into your soul. It teaches you about love, what it is, and sometimes, what it isn't. It shows you your capacity to feel, to give, and even to lose. And though it feels like it breaks you, it also reveals the strength you didn't know you had. Heartbreak teaches you about resilience, ability to stand back up when life knocks you down. It teaches you about boundaries, about how much of yourself you can give before it's too much. It teaches you self-respect, and also that your worth doesn't depend on someone else's love, actions or behaviour. The pain you're feeling right now is temporary. But it's shaping you, moulding you into someone stronger, someone wiser. It's teaching you patience and empathy, not just for others but for yourself as well. And most importantly heartbreak teaches you that you can survive even after losing someone you thought you couldn't live without. And one day when you will finally step into that light at the end of the tunnel, which you will certainly, you'll look back and realize that the heartbreak wasn't a punishment, it was a gift. A hard gift, yes, but a valuable one. It prepared you for what's ahead, for the kind of love, life, and peace you truly deserve. So let heartbreak guide you, not define you. Let it teach you what you need to know, so when you're ready, you can step forward into a brighter, stronger, and more hopeful version of yourself.

See when you are going through heartbreak and you're in the middle of it, love can feel like a cruel joke, a promise that was broken, or a dream that slipped through your fingers. But as much as heartbreak hurts, it also gives you a rare opportunity to pause, to reflect, and most importantly, to redefine what love means to you. You see, when you're in the thick of it, it's easy to let the pain overshadow everything else. But this is the time to ask yourself what is love, really? And redefine what love for you is. Love is not just about someone else completing you. That's the first thing heartbreak can teach you. So while you're healing, take this time to look inward. Reflect on the love you gave. Was it unconditional, or were you sacrificing too much of yourself? These questions might be hard to face, but they're necessary. They help you understand what love should be moving forward. Redefining love also means turning some of that love inward. We're so quick to give our love away to others. But what about giving it to ourselves? Love yourself the way you wanted them to love you. So, as you heal, remember that heartbreak isn't just about letting go of the past. It's about understanding that love isn't perfect, but it should always be real. And the most important love story you'll ever have is the one you write with yourself.

Life has a way of teaching us the hardest lessons through the things we can't control. And heartbreak, whether it's the end of a relationship or a dream that has been shattered is one of those lessons. No matter how much you try to hold on, to fix, or to fight, there comes a point when you realize that some things are simply out of your hands. A breakup is like a storm. It's wild, intense, and unforgiving. It comes out of nowhere, uprooting everything you thought was secure. You may want to calm it, to stop the rain, to make the winds disappear. But the truth is, you can't. The thing about heartbreak is it demands acceptance. What comes after the storm is what matters most. The air feels fresher, the world looks clearer. You realize that you're still here, still standing, and that's not a small thing.

The hope and the light that's waiting for you at the end of the tunnel isn't just about the absence of pain. It's about new you, your strength, and your ability to move forward. It's about understanding that while you couldn't control the storm. So, let the storm come. Let it rage, let it do its worst. But know that it will pass. And when it does, you'll step into the light not as the same person who went through the heartbreak, but as someone stronger, wiser. Because life still has a lot to offer.

Remember: *So wherever you are in this tunnel, keep going. The tunnel has an end, and the light is closer than you think.*

4) Happiness

Happiness is something we all desire, right? We chase happiness in different ways: through success, relationships, adventures, or even in the simple pleasure of a good cup of coffee. But what exactly is happiness? Is it a feeling? A goal? Or something much deeper? We hear about happiness all the time like "You deserve to be happy!" "Happiness is the key to life!" But when it comes down to it, nobody really know what really happiness is?

Happiness is one of those things that seems simple, but the more we think about it, the more complicated it becomes. You might wonder "Why does happiness matter so much?" The truth is, happiness impacts almost every area of our lives. When we're happy, we feel healthier, more energized, and more connected to the people around us. We make better choices, we are more creative, and we handle life's challenges with more ease. Happiness doesn't just make life more enjoyable but it also it enhances our well-being and helps us grow as individuals.

In this section, we're going to take a journey into the heart of happiness. We'll explore what it truly means, why it doesn't always come from external sources like money or fame, and how it can be cultivated from within.

I) What is Happiness?

Before we talk about the definitions and meanings of happiness, have you ever stopped to ask yourself, "What does happiness really mean?" It's one of those words we all know well, and yet, when we try to define it, it can feel a bit tricky. We all want to be happy, right? But how do we truly understand what happiness is?

At first, happiness might seem simple like feeling good, right? Maybe it's the joy you feel when you're with your favourite person or the excitement you get from accomplishing something big. But happiness isn't just about those moments of excitement or pleasure. It's deeper than that.

In this section, we'll break down what happiness really means. We'll explore how it's not just about fleeting moments of pleasure but also about how we feel about our lives as a whole. Happiness isn't a destination – it's a journey, and it can look different for each of us. By understanding what happiness truly is, we can start creating more of it in our own lives. So, what is happiness for you? Let's dive in and explore this important question together. You might find that the answer isn't as far out of reach as you think.

We all know that happiness has many faces, right? It can look different for everyone, it can be a laugh with friends, a quiet moment of peace, or the rush of excitement when you achieve something. But if we strip it down to its simplest form, the basic meaning of happiness is life happening in a more vibrant, energetic, and joyful way than it normally does. It's like when everything around you feels a little brighter, when the ordinary moments are filled with extra sparkle. Think about it for a second sometimes, life just feels... flat. We go through the daily routines wake up, work, eat, sleep and everything feels a bit dull. But happiness is that burst of colour in your day, when something makes you feel alive and connected to the world.

Imagine you're walking down the street on a sunny day, and you suddenly feel the warmth on your skin and hear the birds singing. Everything feels a little more alive, right? You might even smile for no reason. That's a small, everyday example of happiness showing up in a more exuberant way. It's life being a little more vivid, a little more exciting than it normally is. Happiness is that shift that extra sense of wonder and appreciation for what's around you. Happiness is not about waiting for the big moments. It's about recognizing and cherishing the moments that make your life feel full, alive, and worth living. Because when we're happy, we see things through a different lens we notice the beauty, the possibilities, and the joy in the present. So, at its core, happiness is life showing up with more energy, more feelings, and more colours than the usual.

Another mistake many of us make when it comes to happiness is thinking that it's all about money, fame, or power.

We believe that once we achieve those things a big pay check, recognition, or status we'll finally be happy. We imagine that these external achievements will bring us lasting joy, and once we get them, everything will fall into place. But many people who have reached those very things celebrities, business tycoons, and influencers have openly shared that they're not as happy as we might think. They've got the money, the fame, the power, but something is still missing. They feel empty, lonely, or even lost. Why is that? Because happiness isn't something that can be bought or earned through titles or wealth. Sure, these things can bring temporary satisfaction or excitement. They might make life a bit easier or more comfortable in some ways, but they don't guarantee long lasting happiness.

When we place all our focus on external achievements like money, fame, or power, we end up chasing something that's always just out of reach. The more we get, the more we think we need. It's like trying to fill a cup with water that has a hole in the bottom no matter how much we pour in, it never stays full. So, what does this mean for us? Well it's just a reminder for you that happiness can't be found in the things we think we want. It's about finding contentment in what we already have, focusing on the simple joys, and building our happiness from within. True happiness comes from how we live our lives. Don't get me wrong having money, fame, and power isn't a bad thing. They can bring opportunities and open doors. But they shouldn't be the end goal in your life. True happiness comes from creating a life that feels meaningful, connected, and true to who we are. And that's something no amount of money or fame can give us.

Now, let's jump into my definition of happiness, how I see it. To me, happiness is simply a state of mind. It's not something that depends on what's happening around us or on the things we have. And I think one of the most important things you should realize about happiness is that it has nothing to do with the external world. It's all about how we choose to think and feel in any given moment.

Here's an example to help explain what I mean: Let's say something great happens, like a promotion at work or winning a prize. Now, two people could experience the exact same event, and one could be absolutely overjoyed while the other might not feel happy at all. Why is that? Because happiness is personal. It's based on how each individual interprets the situation, how they view the world, and what their mind-set is. For instance, one person might see a promotion at work as a dream come true, a sign that all their hard work has paid off, and they feel proud and excited. But another person might feel stressed or even unhappy about it because he might feel that he deserved more. And that's because happiness is not about the event itself; it's about how we respond to it. This idea really shifts the way we can think about happiness. It means we're not at the mercy of external circumstances. We don't need to wait for the "perfect" job, the "perfect" relationship, or the "perfect" situation to be happy. Happiness is about how we choose to frame our experiences and how we decide to feel about them.

The key takeaway here is that happiness is different for everyone because it's shaped by our individual thoughts, feelings, and perceptions. What makes one person happy might not even move the needle for someone else. It's all about how we look at life and what we choose to focus on. The more we realize this, the more empowered we become to create our own happiness regardless of what's happening in the outside world.

So, if you ever feel like happiness is something out of your reach, remember: it's not something that depends on your circumstances. It's always within you, waiting for you to tap into it. Shift your mind-set and choose to see the good, the joy, and the possibilities in your life. Because happiness is a state of mind you can be happy anytime, anywhere.

Here's something really important I want you to understand, don't expect yourself to be happy all the time. I know it sounds strange because we often think that happiness means being in a constant state of joy and excitement. But the truth is, you can't be happy all the time, and that's completely okay. Life is full of ups and downs, and happiness isn't about feeling "up" every second of the day.

Happiness, in my view, has two main forms: pleasure and joy. Both are important, but they're very different from each other. Pleasure is the fun, exciting, or indulgent part of happiness.

It's the quick burst of happiness you feel when you eat your favourite food, go on a fun trip, or buy something new. It's great when it happens, but it doesn't last forever. The thrill of getting what you want or having something new fades, and that's normal.

Now, joy is different. Joy is deeper and more lasting. It's the kind of happiness that doesn't depend on external things. Joy comes from within, from appreciating life as it is, from finding peace in the present moment, and from living in alignment with what truly matters to you.

If you think you can always have pleasure, then you are fooling yourself and setting up for disappointment. Life is not like that, there will be moments of pleasure, yes, but there will also be times when things are harder, when you feel down, or when things don't go your way. And that's okay. The key is not to expect constant pleasure but to understand that joy is already here. Joy comes from recognizing that life is beautiful, even in its imperfections. Life is in the small moments, the quiet times, just be present and grateful for whatever you have. This understanding means "waking up." When you realize that joy doesn't depend on chasing next thing or waiting for your life to be perfect.

So, stop expecting yourself to be happy all the time. Instead, focus on finding joy in the moments, in the people, in the small things that make life meaningful. Pleasure will come and go, but real joy, deep joy is always there, waiting for you to recognize it. And when you do, that's when you truly start living.

Now to wrap things up about happiness, let's take a moment to think about something Lord Krishna said in bhagavad gita:

$$\text{"कर्मण्येवाधिकारस्ते मा फलेषु कदाचन।}$$
$$\text{मा कर्मफलहेतुर्भुर्मा ते संगोऽस्त्वकर्मणि॥ "}$$

In simple words, he's telling us: "You have the right to perform your actions, but you have no control over the results. Don't be attached to the outcome of your work, and do not let the desire for results distract you from doing what needs to be done. This is such a powerful lesson when it comes to understanding happiness. Many of us chase happiness by focusing too much on the end result. We believe that once we achieve a certain goal, make more money, or find success, we will be happy. But the truth is, happiness doesn't always come from the end goal. It's about the journey the daily steps we take, the moments we experience, and how we feel along the way.

So, when you wake up every day, don't get caught up in what might happen tomorrow. Don't tie your happiness to an outcome you can't control. Instead, focus on the present moment. Enjoy the simple things, a conversation with a friend, a walk in nature, a cup of tea, or the quiet peace of just being alive. Happiness isn't something that will suddenly appear once you achieve your dreams. It's something you can experience every day, if you choose to look for it.

Remember happiness is in the everyday in the small, meaningful moments that make up your life. So, take a step back, breathe, and know that happiness is always there, within you, as long as you choose to embrace it in each moment.

Remember: *In the end, happiness isn't something you chase after. Happiness is something you create by how you choose to live, how you see the world, and how you live the journey of life itself.*

II) You are the Source of Your Own Happiness.

(No one else can make you truly happy unless you choose to be.)

Happiness is something we all search for something we all chase. But the truth is, happiness comes from within you. Happiness is not something that others can give you, nor can it be taken away by others.

See nobody else is responsible for our happiness. Only we are responsible for our own happiness. How we feel and react to life depends on our mind-set. If we choose to focus on the good things in life, even when things are tough, we can find happiness. The people around us, or the things we own, may influence how we feel for a moment, but true happiness comes from within, from our own attitude and decisions. Nobody else can make you happy or sad unless you give them that power. It's up to you to look at life with a positive perspective, to learn from challenges, and to appreciate the small joys. The more you realize that your happiness is in your hands, the more freedom and peace you will feel.

Remember, you don't need to wait for the perfect moment or perfect circumstances to be happy. You can start right now by choosing to focus on the good, by being grateful for what you have, and accepting yourself just as you are. Once you understand that your happiness is within you, life becomes a lot more fulfilling.

I feel when we seek happiness in the world, it's like chasing something that keeps slipping away. You might think that if you just get that dream job, buy a new car, or go on a fancy vacation, then you'll finally feel happy. But here's the thing, those feelings of happiness don't last. The excitement fades, and you're left with wanting more. This is because external things, no matter how good they seem at the moment, can't give you lasting happiness. The real secret to long-lasting happiness is to discover it within yourself. It's not about what you own, where you go, or who you're with. True happiness comes from how you see yourself and the world around you. It's about finding peace in who you are, not in what you have. When you learn to be content and at peace with yourself, then that happiness that you find within yourself doesn't fade away no matter what's happening around you.

See if you always rely on outside things or people to make you happy, you're always going to be chasing something that's just out of reach. But when you discover happiness inside of you, through self-acceptance, gratitude, and a positive outlook then it becomes a part of who you are. It's not something that can be taken away, and it also doesn't disappear as soon as the excitement wears off. Instead, it stays with you, no matter of the circumstances.

So, rather than looking for happiness in the outside world, try turn inward. Look at the good things you already have, focus on what makes you feel good about yourself, and appreciating the present moment. The happiness that comes from within you is lasting, and it's always there, waiting for you to embrace it.

To be happy within yourself is just simple process, you don't need to do anything special or extra to feel happy. All you really have to do is stop doing the things that make you feel sad or unhappy. It's not about adding something to your life, but rather removing the things that bring you down. As I said earlier, happiness is already inside of you, waiting to be noticed. It's your negative thoughts, stressful situations, and habits that block it from shining through. All you have to do is you need to stop holding on to things that bring you sadness. When you stop focusing on the things that stress you out or make you feel angry, unhappy, or worried, happiness naturally fills that space. It's like cleaning out a room. The more you clear out the clutter, the more light and fresh air can come in.

For example, if you constantly worry about what others think about you, or if you keep holding onto your past mistakes, then these things will only bring you down. But if you let go of these worries and forgive yourself, then you will create room for happiness. You see, we often make happiness harder than it needs to be, because we constantly focus on all the things that aren't working in our lives. We often think that we need something more—more money, more success, and more things. But in reality, this things may not bring you happiness.

Remember happiness is right here while you're enjoying a good meal, laughing with friends, or just feeling at peace with yourself. It's not about getting somewhere, it's about stopping the things that pull you away from feeling good.

One thing you must understand is that you can't acquire happiness but you can BE happiness and you do that by being kind, forgiving, and compassionate not just to others, but to yourself. And here's the magic of it: when you become happiness, it doesn't just stay with you. It flows out of you and touches the people around you. A smile, a kind word, a helping hand they may seem small, but they can create ripples of happiness that spread far beyond what you can imagine. So try being happiness. Wake up each day and ask yourself, "How can I bring joy to this moment?" Start by being grateful for what you have. Appreciate the little things, like a warm cup of coffee, a sunny day, or the laughter of a loved one. Happiness increases when you share it with others it's not something that you hold; it's something you give. And when you give it freely, it multiplies. By being happiness you become a source of light for yourself and also for everyone you meet.

Now the most important truth about happiness is this: it's about learning how to live with yourself. Think about it no matter where you go or what you do, there's one person you can never escape that person is YOU. From the moment you wake up to the moment you fall asleep, you're with yourself. And here's the thing if you're not at peace with who you are, no amount of success, money, or relationships will ever make you truly happy. By learning to live with yourself I am trying say that accept who you are, flaws and all. Be okay with all your imperfections and know that you don't have to be perfect to be worthy of love and happiness.

The only true place where you can find fulfilment is within yourself. Why? Because external things are temporary. People come and go. Possessions lose their shine. But the relationship you have with yourself? That stays with you forever.

So, how do you learn to live with yourself? Start by getting to know yourself. Spend time alone, not in loneliness, but in self-discovery. Figure out what makes you happy? What are your values? What are the things that light up your soul? The more you understand yourself, the more you can align your life with what truly matters to you. Be someone who always has it together. Embrace who you are your strengths, your quirks and treat yourself with kindness, patience, and understanding. Basically do all the things that you love so that you will love your own company. Because if you don't love being with yourself, how can you expect anyone else to? See the relationship that you have with yourself sets the foundation for every other relationship in your life. So start today. Do the things that bring you joy, that make you grow, that help you feel proud of who you are. Because when you love your own company, the world will love it too.

At the end, the world may try to tell you that happiness is out there somewhere in a job, a relationship, or a new adventure. But those are illusions, temporary fixes that will always leave you wanting more. The truth is simple yet profound happiness has been with you all along. It's not hiding in some faraway place its right there, inside you, waiting to be discovered. It's in the way you choose to see the world, the gratitude you feel for the little things, and the kindness you show to yourself and others.

So start today. Take a deep breath and remind yourself that the only person you truly need to find happiness with is yourself. And when you find that peace within, you'll see that it's not just enough it's everything.

Remember: *Remember the happiness you've been searching for has been with you all along. All you have to do is let it shine.*

III) Contentment

*(The happiest people are not those who have the most,
but those who need the least.)*

In a world driven by ambitions, competitions, and the endless pursuit of more, contentment often feels like a forgotten virtue. We are constantly told to chase the next big goal, to desire a better version of ourselves and our lives. I know that striving for growth and goals is important, but there is an equally valuable quality that grounds us and brings true peace and that quality is contentment.

Contentment is a simple, it means being at peace with where you are and what you have in life. It's learning to see the blessings around us, even when things don't go as planned. As we begin this journey, let me remind you a simple truth: contentment is not found in having everything but in appreciating what we already have.

Even though happiness and contentment are often used interchangeably, but they are not the same. Happiness is often associated with external events or achievements. It can be fleeting, it comes in bursts and fades when the moment passes. Contentment, on the other hand, is deeper. It is not tied to a single event or thing but is a state of being.

Contentment is a quiet, steady feeling of peace and satisfaction that comes from within. It's not about what you have or what you achieve, but about accepting life as it is. While happiness often depends on circumstances, contentment thrives despite them. Happiness brings colour and excitement, while contentment gives us the strength to battle with life's ups and downs with grace and ease.

Even though our emotions are not steady but still they are integral part of our lives, they are the colours that paint our lives. Happiness lights up our world like the warm glow of sunrise, sadness washes over us like a heavy rain, and excitement rushes through us like the thrill of a roller coaster. But if you look closely, you'll see that these emotions, no matter how powerful, are fleeting. They come and go like waves on the shore. Happiness, as wonderful as it feels, doesn't last forever. The things that once brought us joy can lose their charm. Sadness, too, while overwhelming, eventually fades, just like clouds that eventually part to reveal the sun. Even excitement, with all its intensity, burns brightly but briefly, leaving us seeking our next spark.

So now, my question is, if our emotions are so fleeting, what can we hold on to? The answer lies not in chasing emotions, but in finding peace.

See peace is different. It's not a fleeting feeling that comes and goes; it's a state of being, a deep rooted calm that stays with you, no matter the storms that rage around you. When you find peace, you will discover that the world no longer has the power over you. Happiness becomes sweeter, sadness less daunting, and excitement more meaningful because you are anchored. Peace is not about avoiding life's ups and downs but about embracing them with a steady heart. It's the realization that you don't need to control everything or hold on too tightly. Life will always be unpredictable, but when you are at your peace, you accept its ebb and flow without losing your sense of self.

And here's the beautiful thing, peace brings contentment. So, instead of chasing happiness or avoiding sadness, focus on cultivating peace. Sit with yourself, embrace the stillness, and listen to the quiet wisdom within. In peace, you will find the unshakable strength to face life's ever-changing tides with grace. Because once you find peace, you don't just survive life but you truly live it.

Contentment always lies in the present moment or even it's fair to say everything lies in the present moment. Living in the present means letting go of the worries of the future and the regrets of the past. The future is unknown, and the past is unchangeable, but the present moment? That's where life happens. It's where your power lies. When you focus on the here and now, you free yourself from the chains of "what ifs" and "if only's." You begin to notice the beauty that's already around you, the warmth of the sun on your skin, the laughter of a loved one, the quiet comfort of simply being. Even in life's imperfection, there's always something to be grateful for and to be happy about. Gratitude is the bridge that connects you to contentment. When you take a moment to acknowledge the good in your life, no matter how small, you shift your perspective.

Think about the things you often overlook, the meals you eat, the roof over your head, the people who care for you, the ability to breathe and experience life. These are not small things, they're the foundation of your existence and gratitude helps you see them as the blessings. Showing gratitude is more than just saying "thank you." It's a mind-set, a way of living. It's about pausing to appreciate a kind gesture, savouring a moment of peace, or smiling at a simple joy. And when you live with gratitude, you stop waiting for some future moment to make you happy. You realize you already have reasons to be happy, right here, right now. Contentment doesn't mean settling for less or giving up on dreams. It means finding peace in the journey while working toward your goals.

So, take a deep breath. Look around you. There are so many small things that brings you joy, people who make your life worthwhile, and so many things you might have taken for granted. Show gratitude for it all. Because when you live in the present and appreciate what you have, you unlock the secret to true contentment.

At the heart of contentment lies a simple yet profound truth, you are enough, just as you are. You don't need to prove your worth to anyone or strive endlessly for perfection to feel valued. The moment you know yourself fully, your strengths, flaws, and everything in between then you unlock a powerful realization, the life you live is yours to create. We often chase achievements, possessions, or relationships, thinking they will fill a void within us. But the truth is, no external thing can give you the lasting peace you seek. Contentment begins the moment you stop searching outside and turn inward. Once you realize that you are the creator of your life, everything will change. You may not control everything that happens to you, but you have the power to decide how you respond. Choose to focus on growth rather than fear, build a life that aligns with your values, and to let go of what no longer serves you.

This self-awareness leads you to contentment because it shifts your focus from what you lack to what you can build. Instead of feeling powerless, you feel capable. Instead of dwelling on what went wrong, you look forward to what you can make right. Contentment isn't about having a perfect life; it's about knowing that you have everything you need within you to create a meaningful one. It's the peace that comes from accepting yourself fully.

At last: Just like happiness, contentment is a way of being. It's about living in the present moment, showing gratitude for what you have, and believing in your own worth. It's about understanding that life will always have ups and downs, but your inner peace doesn't have to waver.

Remember: *Remember, contentment is about how you feel within. It's about appreciating what we have, embracing the present moment, and finding peace in who we are. When we stop chasing happiness in the outside world and start nurturing it from within, we discover that contentment was always within our reach. The True wealth is not in riches, but in a heart that is at peace with what it has.*